Prosecco

Prosecco

The Wine and the People Who Made It a Success

Luigi Bolzon

Translated by Stephen Parkin

ALMA BOOKS

ALMA BOOKS LTD
3 Castle Yard
Richmond
Surrey TW10 6TF
United Kingdom
www.almaclassics.com

Prosecco first published in Italian by Alma Books Ltd in 2015
This edition first published by Alma Books Ltd in 2019

Luigi Bolzon asserts his moral right to be identified as the author of this work in accordance with the Copyright, Designs and Patents Act 1988

Text © Luigi Bolzon, 2019

Translation © Stephen Parkin, 2019

Jacket design © nathanburtondesign.com
Jacket author photo © Orlando Bonaldo

Photographic portraits of Daniela Franchini, Lucio Altana, Paolo Mancassola, Luigi Colazzo, Pasquale Sarpi, Roberto Gardetto, Roberto Simeone, Roger Nyeko and Teo Catino
© Orlando Bonaldo

Printed in Great Britain by CPI Group (UK) Ltd, Croydon CR0 4YY

ISBN: 978-1-84688-462-7

Contents

Foreword

The success of Prosecco is the result of intuition and creativity working not with the sophisticated techniques of marketing but driven by a human and patriotic desire to impress. It has been one of the most significant episodes among the many which make up the phenomenon known as "Made in Italy".

In the world market for sparkling wines, dominated by the unassailable reputation and large sales of champagne, and the success of cava, for decades Italy was known for Asti Spumante.

These are wines which are distinguished rivals, but with characteristics that are quite different from those we find in Prosecco. The originality of Prosecco has given it a well-established fame and made it dominant in terms of worldwide sales.

Among all those who pioneered Prosecco and worked together to win international recognition for the wine, I'd like to single out two names: the Mionetto family and Luigi Bolzon.

In January 1989 I became the commercial director for the Mionetto firm, and shortly afterwards I had the good fortune to meet Luigi. Over the next few years the firm became the leading producers of Prosecco in the region of Valdobbiadene.

I can still recall the passion and enthusiasm with which all of us worked in those years, as well as Luigi's personal commitment as he travelled the world with a bottle of Prosecco always in his case.

His book vividly brings back to me the episodes, anecdotes and experiences he relates; it is not an academic study of the rise of Prosecco as a historical phenomenon, but an act of love and gratitude towards the many people who played their part in that success and whom he describes here in all their humanity.

— Dino Maule

Prosecco

The Wine and the People Who Made It a Success

FOR ELENA, STELLA, SILVIA

The iconic Prosecco bottle with a "string" design

Introduction

The arrival of Prosecco in Great Britain has followed the same routes as Parmigiano Reggiano and pasta. The energy and entrepreneurial spirit of Italian immigrants, devoted to good food and to the restaurant business, has led to British familiarity with these products and to their being now readily available in places far removed from where they are produced. Whereas the French have traditionally relied on a business model involving sophisticated sales techniques to disseminate their own brands,* the imports of Italian food in Great Britain have been the work of innumerable individual Italians living in the UK. In telling the story of the marketing of Prosecco in Great Britain, the purpose of this book is to recount the various episodes and views of the last thirty years, to record the human and professional experiences of the main characters who were involved, and to capture their attitudes and sensibilities through their own accounts and reminiscences. The general outlines which emerge will help us to better understand the remarkable success story of the trade in Prosecco.

Author's preface

This story began with a promise I made to the Italian owner of a London restaurant. I told him I would write something about the way Italian restaurateurs had promoted Prosecco and other Italian food products. One day he'd said to me: "Nobody writes about us and the contribution we make to Italian exports. The politicians and the institutions take all the praise for the work that is done by us." "Don't worry," I told him unhesitatingly, "I'll take care of that." He smiled: "But are you up to writing something?" I replied: "I've never done any – but then again, what did you know about running a restaurant before you owned one?"

My love of Prosecco started at the end of the 1970s, when I was studying in Venice. In those days, before the lectures in the morning we usually had breakfast in a bar – a cappuccino and a warm brioche. But I suffered from digestive problems, and my friend Angelo Pigatto thought that drinking cappuccinos might be causing them, so instead of the traditional Italian breakfast I took to drinking a glass of Prosecco and eating a *tramezzino*, the kind of sandwich you find in Venetian bars, made with soft bread and with different kinds of fillings. My digestion improved, and I started to sing the praises of Prosecco. In it I had identified something which benefited body, mind and heart.

In the second half of the 1980s I moved to England, as a result of a day I'd spent at the seaside with my friend Ruggero Ragagnin. Two German girls had complained about the fact that neither of us spoke a word of English. So I got in the car and set off north. My impressions of the country, once I'd crossed the Channel, were conflicting. I stayed in Blackpool to do an intensive language course. The teacher spoke to us of the differences between residents of London, where more foreigners lived, and those who lived in the rest of the United Kingdom. He declared that "immigrants bring a lot of benefits to our island. Thanks to the children of mixed marriages, they also improve the appearance of the native population."

As far as food was concerned, I'd been warned not to get my hopes up. British people ate fried fish and chips, wrapped in newspaper, with their hands: the printing ink was just another dressing, like the salt and vinegar. They ate at every conceivable hour of the day, in buses and trains, standing or walking, or even while driving. I grimaced every time bad cooking smells wafted past me. Untrained and unqualified staff handled food and drink with hardly any attention to basic hygienic norms.

Dating a woman in Britain also worked differently. Offering a drink – gin and tonic, or whisky and Coke – to the girls you met in a local pub was a sure-fire way to get their attention. But the sheer kindness of the people of Lancashire pushed my reservations about eating British food and meeting British girls into second place. If you find yourself in difficulties, the Brits will respond with their usual good manners, asking: "How can I help you?" In the Veneto I couldn't recall such helpfulness ever being shown to strangers. I admired the sense of civic responsibility, the respect shown by drivers for the highway code and for pedestrians, and I was amused by the self-deprecation and humorous outlook of English people. Public administration works well in Great Britain, and, collectively, the British seem more efficient than Italians, who are forced to adapt to the disorganization of their public services by cultivating independent-minded inventiveness, and who therefore come across as more autonomous.

But six months weren't enough to become familiar with the new language, so I decided to stay on in the country and find work – a job connected to Treviso and Prosecco.

Gianni Segatta, in describing his own experiences, confirms the problems foreigners used to face in the old days in trying to adapt to British ways:

"After the obligatory spell of military service, I moved to London in 1967, because there were openings for people like me with a diploma from an agricultural college. I already had a contract in my pocket when I got on the train. I was going to work with the bottling and distribution of wine, since in that period in the British market wine was imported in barrels and bottled in the UK. Several Italian friends had described my destination to me in glowing terms, so I arrived at my lodgings full of anticipation. However, the reality fell short of my expectations. At the sight of those filthy rooms,

I wanted to take the train straight back home. But my sense of pride won out. I cleaned the rooms and changed the sheets on the bed. When I'd finished cleaning, I went out to eat. Unappetizing smells emerged from every restaurant door. I ate at Papà Piccolino's on London's Goodge Street, where no one spoke Italian. From that day on I decided to cook my own meals at home. I enrolled in a language school on Charlotte Street and started to invite the new people I met back for dinner as a matter of course: in my parents' home in Trento it was normal for me to eat lunch and dinner with my brothers and sisters, my aunts and other family friends, all welcomed in by my mother Albertina, who was a very good cook. Eating on my own just felt wrong to me."

PART ONE

"The growth of interest in Prosecco outside Italy was down to ordinary men who were gifted with a spontaneous entrepreneurial flair that found an outlet in concrete action. The arrival of Prosecco in Great Britain should be seen against the backdrop of this complex process of emigration and, along with this, the spread of typical Italian food and drink." (Luigi Bolzon)

The spirit of Italian emigration in the United Kingdom

Over the course of the nineteenth century, along with other Italian emigrants,* political exiles, inspired by their constitutional ideals and intent on undermining the ruling governments in Italy, arrived in Great Britain. They were cultivated scions of the middle classes, and they found work as teachers or in other roles in the cultural ambience of the time. Among these exiles, Garibaldi and Mazzini stand out. Under the influence of Lord Palmerston, at first Foreign Secretary and subsequently Prime Minister, they worked on their plans for national unification while fomenting rebellion in Italy. The second half of the nineteenth century saw waves of immigration from Italy of the poorer classes searching for economic survival, since in the years immediately following unification their conditions at home were unsustainable. "Migrant or brigand" – this expression of the time sums up the state of affairs. As they wandered across Europe on foot, relying on people's charity, the Italian migrants thought up different ways of making ends meet. They sold painted figurines or hot chestnuts on the street, decorated tiles, played street organs or performed acrobatic tricks in public squares. Many of these vagabonds came to settle in the neighbourhood known as Little Italy in Holborn in central London, where there was already a small Italian community. They managed to find humble jobs, while the more inventive among them devised more unusual ways of making a living.

"It was Italian immigrants who introduced ice cream to the British as a street food and who created the thriving takeaway culture that still survives in cities such as Glasgow to this day."*

Some among them, known as "hokey-pokey", sold ice cream. They would wheel a small cart around the streets, introducing passers-by to this novel and delicious treat. At first they served the ice cream in shells or on small plates and glasses. The customer would lick the plate clean and then give it back to the ice-cream seller, who would wash it and use it again. It cost one penny, making it affordable for poorer people, who were thus able to enjoy a treat which until then had been the preserve of the wealthy. The increase in trade attracted many of their fellow countrymen. The expression "hokey-pokey" may have derived from the phrase

"*Ecco un poco*" ("Here's a little bit"), which later became the habitual cry of the ice-cream sellers to attract people's attention. Mario Berzolla has suggested that "the expression, like 'abracadabra', seemed to have magical properties. In the midst of poverty and misery, ice cream was like an apparition conjured up by a spell."

The number of Italians went on growing in the more prosperous parts of Great Britain, the industrial cities of Manchester, Liverpool, Glasgow and Edinburgh, as well as in Wales, whose wealth came from coal and iron mining. Many Italians set up coffee shops, which sold sweets, cigarettes, hot drinks like tea and coffee, and simple snacks. These shops turned into places of welcome, where local people, who had few other opportunities for relaxation, could meet and socialize. Berzolla writes about his family's experiences in Wales:

"My maternal grandfather was called Lazzaro Ricci. In 1921 he left Bardi, a small village in the Apennine mountains in Emilia Romagna. He went to Wales and worked as a waiter for two years before opening his own shop. He died during the Second World War. My father, Lazzaro Berzolla, came from Gravago, a hamlet consisting of five houses close to Bardi. He worked hard and opened his own coffee shop. Before and after the war the Italians didn't meet with much sympathy, but the immigrants from Bardi were mountain folk: they were tough characters, and they knew how to survive. Now things have changed, and the old coffee shops have closed. The children and grandchildren of Italian immigrants like me have gone to school and university, and the prospect of selling fish and chips no longer attracts them. I was seven when my father died, so I didn't know him. If he and my grandfather had lived longer, I could say more about them. But there are lots of Italians from Bardi in Wales, and they all have stories they can tell."

Emilio Nella writes about another unusual job introduced by Italian emigrants: "My great-grandfather, who was called Emilio Nella like me, couldn't read or write. In 1901, because of economic hardship, he left Pinzolo, a small village in the mountains of the Trentino. Others before and after him did the same over a period of bad harvests. With a cart and a grindstone, my great-grandfather set off northwards without a precise destination. He went from town to town sharpening knives in hotel kitchens and butcher's shops. It was the only kind of work he could do – in Pinzolo all he'd ever done was mow fields and sharpen scythes. He usually spent the night in barns belonging to his customers, and more often than not he was given food and drink in lieu of payment. After one long year spent wandering, he arrived on the outskirts of London and settled in Dartford, where he set up his business." Today Emilio junior continues his great-grandfather's business. He's made money; now he drives around in a gleaming grey Bentley, not a cart, owns four houses and is the proud father of five children. "Knife-grinders love children, their families and their work." At the entrance into Pinzolo there's a monument with a statue of a knife-grinder or *moleta*, erected and paid for by donations from emigrants born in the town and now living all over the world.

In June 1940 the Italian Government declared war on Britain, and the Italians who'd settled in the country lost everything they'd built up over years of hard work. Ordinary workers were treated like dangerous criminals; their possessions were requisitioned, and they themselves were put in prison or deported and interned in countries like Canada and Australia. No attempt was made to distinguish between supporters of the Fascist regime, who had antagonized the British population with their propaganda, and those who opposed it. The two countries were at war, and there was no time for such nice distinctions. Among the unfortunate victims, over 400 Italians drowned in the Irish Sea on board the *Arandora Star*, a ship carrying about 1,400 prisoners of war, Germans and Italians.* On 2nd July 1940, at 7 a.m., it was hit by a torpedo launched from a German submarine. One of the victims was Cesidio Di Ciacca, the grandfather of the writer Mary Contini, who, in her book *Dear Olivia*, has written a fictionalized account of the moving episodes associated with the tragedy, imagining a chain of events that was both dramatic and absurd.*

Pietro De Cesare, who works as a food and wine rep, writes of other Italian prisoners of war in this period: "During the war the lucky ones were sent to work as agricultural labourers on the farms of Worcestershire and Warwickshire, where wheat and maize were grown. The labourers were employed on local farms; their aptitude for hard work was highly rated, and they stayed on as workers in this fertile land. They started to cultivate new crops such as aubergines and courgettes."*

After the war was over, the Italians in Great Britain gradually resumed their activities, at the same time seeking out new areas of work. At the end of the 1940s, there was a new wave of Italian immigration into the United Kingdom on the basis of officially agreed plans for what was called "collective recruitment", stipulated between the Italian and British governments, in order to supply manufacturing labour for the host country. The men were sent to work in the mines, steel mills and brick factories, while the women mostly found work in the textile industry. The more enterprising among them, when the opportunity presented itself, set up their own businesses, proving that desperate conditions can also be creatively stimulating, and lead to a silent and constructive social revolution.

The emigrants of the following generations left Italy either out of hardship or because they were dissatisfied with their lot. Like those who had gone before them, they set off on journeys with uncertain destinations. An artisan from Treviso, Luigi Favero, encouraged those who were not sure whether to leave or not by telling them not to try to "plan ahead for difficulties, but tackle them as they crop up". These men and women ventured forth on the road out of necessity; the fear of the unknown did not immobilize them: on the contrary, the unforeseen drove them along. They didn't wait for government help, but took control of their own destinies in distant and unfamiliar countries. The standard advice to young people in post-war Italy was that they should get a degree if they wanted to work in Europe, but the Italian workers just mentioned here prove the contrary. Relying on their own abilities, they made their way in the world and played a fundamental role in the growth of the Italian economy. A degree might help a person to adapt to certain conditions, but it's sheer necessity which leads to action and encourages personal initiative. The protagonists in this story share in common a determination to survive and to live. They were formed in the university of life: it taught them how to improvise, made them open and direct when faced with the new and the unexpected. They were born to distinguish themselves, to stand out from the ordinary run of people. Their freedom of spirit would very probably have been cramped by formal education, which by definition prepares individuals to weigh up carefully the pros and cons and heed others' instructions before embarking on anything. Nicola Foresta – a dealer in wine, cheese and coffee who on his arrival in England anglicized his name to Nick Forest – has observed ironically that "it's hard to imagine Italian expatriates sitting in a classroom". "I'm a complete ignoramus," one Sicilian restaurateur confessed to the food and wine rep Pasquale Cannarile, "but I know how to use my brain." An ignorance of abstract theories and notions can be advantageous for someone who's creative, and increase their energy; these are people who never get stuck in a rut, whose sheer originality at times seems comic and entertaining. "Drive and courage are the qualities you find in individuals who plunge into action and only afterwards take time to reflect": this was how the young Domenico Taravella described himself, and it's true he himself worked like this, throwing himself into activity and embarking on projects by instinct.

No dogs, no Italians

This is how Luigi Marinelli recounts his personal experiences: "In the early 1960s I worked as a waiter in Basle, in Switzerland. I didn't stay long; I didn't feel very welcome as a fellow human being. I remember vividly the sign you sometimes saw outside shops: 'No dogs! No Italians!' But, as Italians, we'd do well to reflect on this sign. Back then some of the Italians in Switzerland didn't behave well – in fact they were outright rogues. They got girls pregnant and then upped it and moved elsewhere. I arrived in Glasgow in 1966; I found the city welcoming and started to work for the Vesuvio restaurant. Years later, I turned to trading in food and wine.

"Lots of Italians ended up in Scotland by mistake. They were planning to go to America, but the ship which was carrying them found it easier to leave them in countries that were nearer. They didn't speak English – they hardly spoke Italian – and it was only after they'd been left that they found out they'd been tricked. The Italian community in Scotland introduced wine and food and a *joie de vivre* to

Scotland, and now the Scottish have a great respect for us.
But at the beginning it was difficult. All the hardest jobs,
those the British don't care to do, were left for the Italians
– but when the Indians and Pakistanis and Polish arrived,
they became the bottom of the pile, while we went up in
the social scale."

The intention in the pages that follow is to give faces and
identities to the army of Italians who came to work in the
United Kingdom and promoted interest in Prosecco. There
are so many who deserve to be remembered, but even with
the best of intentions it will be impossible to name them all.
But perhaps others who've contributed to this story will be
encouraged by these pages to add their own accounts and
complete the picture.

Types of emigrants

The emigrants who left Italy in past centuries in order to
leave behind dismal social conditions were different from
more recent emigrants, who chose to work and live abroad
because they were seeking new economic and entrepreneurial
opportunities. "Emigrant" is in fact not the right word
for someone like the restaurant owner Pierluigi Bianchi.
Bianchi is from Milan and is a passionate supporter of
AC Milan. He went to England in 1984 to see the match
between Liverpool and Everton; while there he met and fell
in love with Irene Bagatti, who came from an Italian family
living in the UK. He decided to settle in Kent and open a

restaurant, Pierluigi's, in Beckenham. In 1986 he attended the annual gala organized by Ciao Italia, an association of Italian restaurant owners who were all living and getting on well in the UK. The event was held at the Café Royal in Mayfair; Lord Charles Forte* was present. Forte's family was originally from Ciociaria, in the province of Frosinone; at the time he was the head of Trusthouse Forte, a large chain of hotels and restaurants. Also present at the gala was the then Italian Minister of Agriculture, as well as official representatives from various institutions. While the speech of his British counterpart lasted two minutes, the Italian minister, speaking in Italian, went on and on. Pierluigi reports that "others tried to signal to him that he should try to wrap it up, because there were other speakers waiting their turn". With the usual populist rhetoric, the minister began by addressing the "poor emigrants, forced to leave [their] homeland…" Pierluigi exchanged glances with Franco Santoro,* who was sitting next to him, and whispered: "What's he on about? They're all millionaires here and getting on very nicely in the UK, thank you very much." Pierluigi does not agree with the connotation of the word "emigrant" in Italian. "The pity for emigrants comes from what Italians feel for the foreigners who come to their country and find a State incapable of integrating them into society. For me, living in England was a choice, not a necessity; I preferred to live here rather than in Italy. So I'm not an emigrant in the accepted historical significance of the term. In the context of contemporary society, I'm working as part of the European common market. I've made my choices freely. Here people pay their taxes and obey the rules, and they respect and enjoy their rights as citizens." Pierluigi's heartfelt remarks should make us careful about the way we use the word "emigrant" in future.

There have been many different reasons over the centuries for Italians leaving their homeland. And they've left in many different ways: on foot, riding bicycles or motorbikes, by car, hitch-hiking, on trains and planes. Irene, Peter and Steven Bagatti's paternal grandfather, Giovanni Bagatti, from the village of Bardi, made his way to England on foot at the beginning of the twentieth century. He carried a gold coin with him as a kind of passport or *laissez-passer* to show to the customs people at Dover, as a proof he could support himself in his adopted country. In those days emigrants carried with them other forms of currency, such as sterling banknotes their relatives already in Britain had posted to them. Gerardo Coppola,* who emigrated from Italy in the 1970s out of necessity, tells his story: "I left Salerno with two sweaters and two pairs of trousers and without a single lira in my pocket. After a period working in Venice, followed by a spell in Munich and then Geneva, I went to England." The restaurant owner Pasquale Sarpi left Crotone to avoid doing military service (though his father Umberto could boast he'd served for four years in the navy). Giuseppe Turi went to London in 1982 after working with friends in the Puglian countryside and setting up an agricultural cooperative intended to recultivate land which had been abandoned. "We wanted to change the world, but unfortunately – or perhaps it was a stroke of good luck – the local circumstances were against us." Someone from the Veneto reflects on what drove him to emigrate: "I feel like a vagabond, a permanent migrant. I left a secure job because I thought travelling round the world would settle my youthful restlessness and all its problems. I still haven't reached my goal, but at least I'm still trying." Emanuele Orto* and Giovanni Guerrieri moved to England because of love. Giovanni's – and Janice's – son, Jonathan, tells his parents' story: "My dad is Sicilian, from Ragusa. At the age of nineteen he was doing his military service on board the *Amerigo Vespucci*; in July 1966 the ship called at Venice, and, under the bell tower in St Mark's Square, he met my mother, Janice Woods, who was seventeen and on a summer holiday in Venice. He offered to buy her an ice cream, and they exchanged addresses. They wrote to each other using their own languages; neither understood what the other was saying. Janice asked someone who worked in her local post office and who knew Italian to translate. Then she went to Sicily to spend some time with him. She spent six months living with her future in-laws and learning how to speak in Sicilian dialect. Since there were problems finding work, they decided to move to London, where they got married. Giovanni worked in the Ford car factory, but in the evening, in order to earn extra money so they could save up to buy a house, he was a waiter at the Savoy. With three children to bring up,* my parents opened the Pizzeria Vesuvio,

and then a restaurant called La Notte, and after that they
started a new restaurant, the Amerigo Vespucci. In 1993
they moved the restaurant to the new business district in
Canary Wharf, by the Thames; it reminded them a bit of
where they'd first met. They're both retired now, but still
happily married and enjoying foreign travel and looking
after their grandchildren."

Great Britain and Italian restaurants

The Romans had problems conquering Britain. Not even
Julius Caesar succeeded. The geographical position of the
island, detached from the rest of Europe, has restricted its
contacts with other peoples, making the character of its
inhabitants peculiar. An Italian friend complained to me
that he "has lived in England for forty years and doesn't
have one English person among his friends". The Florentine
restaurant owner Roberto Mangoni remembers going to
his British fiancée's family home for Sunday lunch in the
1960s: "We didn't sit down at a table, but ate standing, like
horses." Though, as it happens, Roberto had developed a
real passion for horses. He was once asked what he would
do if he had to choose between Sheila, his fine Irish wife,
and horses – to which he replied: "It's neck and neck." The
salesman Giorgio Casadei, based on his own experience,
adds that on these occasions "there was never anything to
drink during the meal, and only after it was over were you
offered a cup of tea". Those Italians who bought a house

during this period were puzzled by the British conception of space and interior decoration. There was wall-to-wall carpeting in the sitting room, the bathroom, the kitchen... all the carpeting seemed to imply that British housewives like to wear slippers rather than busying themselves in the kitchen with cooking. By way of contrast, the dining room of an Italian house in the pre-boom years of the 1950s and 1960s – which was often the kitchen, or, in the case of agricultural workers, part of the cowshed, with the cattle in their stalls exuding warmth – always contained a table and chairs, where the whole family would sit down to eat lunch and dinner. A tablecloth covered the table, and there was always wine to drink.* The contrast explains the opinion Italians often have that for the British eating is a mere physiological necessity. Giuseppe Marini, who owns a chain of more than ten restaurants in Scotland (Tony Macaroni), displays an Italian sign on the walls of his restaurants – "Tony Macaroni Lives to Eat" – which indicates the Italian passion for food, unlike the attitude of the British, who eat to live. The foreigners contributed to inspire in the British the pleasures of sitting down around a table to eat. The mission to introduce Italian food was a demanding task, but those who were prepared to put in the effort found rewarding opportunities. They had left a country shackled by a system of "small favours" and found one where by contrast it was easy to set up a business. "I arrived in England at the end of the 1970s," recalls Enzo Di Nolfi, owner of the Raffaella restaurant in Ashford, "to find an appointment with a local bank manager had been set up for me. I went with a friend because I didn't speak any English. The manager showed us into his office and sat us down in front of him. I was really thrilled. He asked me what my plans were. 'I'm a good cook,' I told him. He then asked me if opening a local restaurant was an ambition. After a twenty-minute chat he agreed to give me a loan to enable me to set up a business. The only guarantee he required was the rental contract on the restaurant." "Workers are welcome in Britain. The British are good at organizing the work of others," Lino Della Pesca, the owner of Tiggi's Holdings, remarks. "If it weren't for foreigners creating change, Preston would be lifeless." He adds that "it's thanks to Italian restaurant owners that people, even more than before, go out to eat to celebrate birthdays and other anniversaries, Mother's Day, St Valentine's Day". It was often the case that waiters and maîtres d's managed to buy the restaurant thanks to wealthy clients. They would set up a limited company, and if the main investor decided to pull out, bought up his share. Unfortunately not everyone who succeeded in doing this had the skills to run a business. Taking advantage of the opportunities offered by the British system, many Italians set up their own companies, even though many weren't capable of running their household accounts, let alone a business. It also needs to be said that there were some Italians who'd left Italy after brushes with the law:* members of the Mafia, thieves and smugglers, drug dealers and other such ne'er-do-wells. Many former criminals managed to integrate into British society and abide by the rules, while a small minority continued to cause problems. Roberto Simeone, who works in the hospitality industry,* points out that "even the many films on the Mafia have helped spread knowledge of Italian food". All this in its way has caused confusion, but also created publicity and helped, without actually intending to, the development of foreign markets for Italian products.

Italian exporters still regard the United Kingdom as a complex country. Its distance from Italy and its climate have created ways of life which are very different from those found in Italy. From a historical point of view, the UK was created some time before the Italian nation. Large parts of England are mostly level, with long lines of hills, although the UK as a whole has numerous mountain ranges. However, England's comparatively flat terrain, in contrast to Italy's, has tended to make the inhabitants more uniform in various ways.* A foreign tourist will find the English spoken in different parts of the country different because of the accent, while in Italy someone from the Veneto won't even understand the dialect of someone from the neighbouring region of Friuli.

Towns and cities in Britain look similar: the main streets of the urban centres have the same chains of shops and restaurants. The architect Enrico Sgarbi from Verona – who prefers working in the wine retail trade to being an architect – finds the sight "rather boring".

In the countryside the style of the houses shows a mixture of inventiveness and respect for tradition. The buildings are well integrated into the environment, and the general effect is one of harmony. In Italy the lack of systematic urban planning means that individuals can choose a style of building which is incongruous with the surroundings. In this way individual choice has ruined low-lying areas and city suburbs.

A characteristic style of cooking, gastronomically very limited, survives in the United Kingdom. Young British people are hard put to name more than five of their country's typical dishes, of which one is normally the glorious and internationally famous "English breakfast", served in hotels all over the world, consisting of eggs, bacon, sausages, button mushrooms, baked beans and grilled tomatoes. In Italy, on the other hand, every single region boasts an abundant variety of dishes.

The difficulties that were encountered first in familiarizing the Brits with Prosecco, followed by the easy rapidity with which the taste for it spread, can both be ascribed to the differences between Italy and Great Britain. The Italian attitude to eating and drinking is natural, while the British approach, when it isn't physiological, is academic. When Italians drink a glass of wine, it's enough for them to say it's good: its main function is to be part of the social occasion, to encourage communication. The British analyse the aromas. For an ordinary Italian, drinking wine is just part of the experience of eating. The British Government regards wine as a socially problematic alcoholic beverage, to be taxed like cigarettes. When an Italian cooks a dish, he or she pays attention to the individual ingredients and respects their characteristics. The chef Fausto Pelizzato, from Castelfranco Veneto, who places a high importance on people eating healthily, has described the role of an Italian cook like this: "They need to know their raw materials and express their qualities in the simplest way possible." Fausto's principle holds good both when we look back at the impoverished Italy of the period after the Second World War, when people had to adapt to scarcity, and the wasteful consumerist society it has become now. However, only a few cooks really understand the meaning of "simplicity". "Simple" cooking is by no means easy: you need to know clearly what you want to do, be independent of fashion and work intelligently. It's like asking an individual to develop personality and beauty without resorting to cosmetics or plastic surgery.

British people are more sophisticated and have remained tied to French influences; they mythologize the chef who's capable of creating dishes with a kind of alchemical fantasy and verve. The chef is like some conjuror who produces his masterpieces with a flourish out of a hat.

Restaurant cooking and domestic cooking for the family circle are different but also related. The first is a business. Modern restaurant cuisine is no longer regulated by norms of good sense; it's become like a chemistry lab or, on occasion, an experiment in baroque rhetoric, virtuoso aesthetic displays where the content is minimal. The extravagant techniques and improvised combinations disguise the lack of good natural products and sometimes risk poisoning consumers. The sculpted dishes created by lauded chefs, in which the ingredients, including even fish, are deprived of their intrinsic flavours, only transmit all the tension, irritability and cursing in the kitchen which have gone into their creation. British diners will frequently comment on the attractive appearance rather than the actual tastiness of the dishes they've ordered. Cooking as sculpture has replaced a living cuisine. In actual fact, diners are incapable of genuinely saying what they think of the dish, since they are silently intimidated by so many formalities and feel impelled to kowtow to current fashion. "Cooking in this way is a real pain," says Aldo Cogo, working in his kitchen. How remote it all seems from the love and serenity with which Italian housewives cooked in the past, when there was always lots of time. In Britain the huge number of cooking programmes on the television and the vast number of cookery books which are published show how the British feel the need to follow a method rather than trusting their instincts and cooking just as it comes. Learning a method is a substitute for a lack of passion. So you have endless competitions, call on expert opinion, award points, as if the value of food and wine is just numerical. "It's a way of showing a mass of consumers incapable of judging for themselves what to think," suggests Claudio Compri* – and he adds, in Venetian dialect, "useful for those who know little about eating and drinking." Guides to restaurants and to wines are enormously successful. Cookery lessons are all part of the commercial pitch. Since Italians were already eating well when housewives didn't feel the need to consult cookery books, the thought occurs – and it's worth saying it out loud – that eating well for Italians is a serious matter. It is all to do with good health and involves everyone, rich and poor, educated and unschooled, without distinction. In Antonio D'Alba's view, such a conception of food echoes the ancient Greeks' idea of art: "Art is universal and open to everyone. Beauty – or tastiness in the case of food – has an essence which is recognizable independently, without the aid of critics or commercial media." On the contrary, over the past twenty years British television has taken to presenting Italian food as a kind of comic act, choosing as presenters pseudo-cooks and figures who conform to the stereotype of the slapdash and clownish Italian, who makes people laugh – an image which has nothing to do with food. Turning Italians into figures of fun inevitably diminishes the historical importance of the widespread influence Italian cooking has had on modern cuisine in the UK. Lorenzo Castiglione, owner of the Hurtwood Inn in Peaslake, Surrey, has remarked ironically: "In Italy it's the politicians who're the clowns, not the cooks." The dignity of cooks in Italy held true for a long time, but nowadays even there you find some chefs who've taken to strutting about like actors and second-rate entertainers, trying to show talent they don't possess. Cooking has become a spectacle that is based on an offensive lack of respect for the cook's raw materials. Older generations of Italians, who'd experienced poverty in their life, used to say that some hardship might end up doing us some good.

A celebrated chef has commented that "in the UK, a chef who wants to take part in a television programme must find a media manager with the right contacts. Not every skilled chef is right for the TV camera, and many TV personalities don't know much about food and have only a limited experience of the catering world. Television doesn't really want experienced chefs with a real ability to instruct viewers, but individuals with an interesting background and past – normal types are not required. So programmers want to find personalities who have a history of drug-taking or gambling, who have a lively love life, who are a bit off the rails." These presenters can attract large audiences both in the UK and in Italy, perhaps because the viewers have a secret wish to see the most ordinary people become successful.

British cooking

Andy McLarin, a promoter of food and wine – and educator – has said: "Until the Sixties in Britain families used to sit down together for meals, and people cooked well, with local and national food products. The Seventies saw the advent of cheap frozen American fast food; people gradually forgot about the tradition of cooking and their own culinary identity." In Andy's view, British cooking has got worse since he was a child; he's thinking in particular of Devon, where he lives. Ann Taruschio, who lives in Wales and is an enthusiastic researcher into culinary history, agrees, declaring: "I don't see a way out." She complains about modern cooking, which shows no awareness of the past and reveals how confused its proponents are. Over the last four decades, restaurant cuisine has evolved in gastronomic terms, but the quality of what people in the UK eat hasn't kept pace. The main suppliers of food products offer a vast range, but often of rather mediocre or even dubious quality. There's a lot of variety, but not much which is really good. "What we've got is cuisine ruled by the 'ping' of the microwave," Lynne Platt says. "My grandmother used to buy potatoes, peel and slice them and cook them. Now you can buy them ready-sliced, you put them in the microwave and a few seconds later 'ping!' – they're ready." Simon Foderingham, the owner of the restaurant Simons at Oxfords in Southampton, sums up the situation: "After the '70s we lost the ability to cook." In short, the British handed over the job of cooking, which they regarded as just a manual chore, to the foreigners who came to their country from all over the world.

A distinction should be drawn between what the poorer social classes ate after the war and the diet of the middle and upper classes. Poor people didn't eat much, and they ate badly, while the well-to-do stuffed themselves with good things. There's still an elite class in the UK who show off their superiority in all kinds of ways – in their education, in what they eat, the sports they practise. The restaurants which form part of exclusive clubs select their customers by requesting a large membership fee. In Italy the divisions between what and how different classes eat is less pronounced, while the growth in economic prosperity among the lower classes has led to the preservation and improvement of the cooking they always did.

It's true of course that Italy's climate and geography mean that ingredients for cooking – the vegetables, salads and herbs – are not only of good quality, but also much more various, which in turn has meant that Italian cuisine is highly diversified.

Italian restaurants in the UK

"If a tourist in London asked me to recommend a good Italian or Chinese or French restaurant, there are lots I could suggest. If they asked me which restaurants serve typical British dishes, I wouldn't be able to think of a single one." (Luciano Frelich)

Imports of pasta, charcuterie, cheeses and some wines are said to have started with the arrival of Italian emigrants at the beginning of the twentieth century. Food shops and distributors such as Donatantonio and Terroni in London and Valvona & Crolla in Edinburgh* are evidence of this first phase of colonization. Back then, the consumption of Italian food was very much aimed at the Italian community; as Italians became increasingly integrated into the local populations, so the British acquired Italian tastes in food and started to buy their products. But it was a long and tortuous process, which began with the very first emigrants; looking back from the current situation, their contribution should not be underestimated.

In terms of food, the UK is an Italian colony. Pizza, pasta, tiramisu, which are now more popular than many traditional British dishes, were all first put on the menu by Italian restaurant owners. The presence of Prosecco in the UK is also down to the men and women who worked in the Italian restaurant business: they were the first to understand its value and potential, and learnt how to tackle the challenges of the markets in the '80s and '90s, when the first strategies to introduce and sell the wine started. After years of slow growth, Prosecco became popular thanks to the efforts of figures that are often underestimated or forgotten, since the laws of the market favour the opportunists, who know how to exploit an advantageous turn of events at the right moment.

> *"Italian restaurateurs in Britain were lucky, because, while the Brits didn't have the same degree of appreciation of food and drink that they had, they were, on the other hand, willing to try something different."*
> (Lino Della Pesca)

Italian restaurants have been active in the UK since just after the Second World War. There were restaurants before then which served a few Italian dishes, but what was missing was confident and enthusiastic migrants to promote the identity and potential of Italian cuisine. Most of the Italian migrants then working in the catering sector had left Italy because of impoverishment, and their knowledge of food was limited because of the privations they'd endured. The professionals started to come in the late 1950s. Giuliano Ferrari, looking back on his own experience, recalls: "In the 1950s and 1960s it was difficult to get into the UK. You needed to be skilled. Trained chefs and waiters came to Britain, like me, because they needed to learn English to find work in major hotels all over the world." Generally speaking, what we think of today as Italian cuisine has developed over the last sixty years, after Italian migrants started to come in the post-war period to work as waiters in restaurants and hotels. Lorenzo Berni, who runs the Osteria San Lorenzo, says of these arrivals after the war: "We'd been defeated in the war, so we had to ask forgiveness. It was this attitude which gave us the humility to accept unskilled jobs." But subsequently Italians learnt how to seize the opportunity to open up their own restaurants. Despite all this, the spread of Italian food in the UK was a lot less easy than looking back from today's vantage point would lead one to believe. Tina Bagatti, of the Trattoria Italiana in Croydon, remembers how, back in the 1950s, "the staff of the Steak House in Notting Hill, where I was working with my husband Aldo, used to have to eat spaghetti in hiding, because the clients didn't like the look of those platefuls of worms". At the beginning of the 1970s, Lino Della Pesca decided to set out for the north of

England with the plan of setting up restaurants and casinos. On the boat from Italy to England, an English lord asked him where he was going, and Lino told him: Harrogate. "Oh no, no, no!" the Englishman replied. "You must always remember that outside London there's just countryside." The warning remained with Lino ever afterwards. On the day his first restaurant opened, a customer ordered *pasta alla carbonara*. The chef had to come and break a raw egg in front of him over the pasta: the menu had said there were eggs in the dish, but the customer claimed he couldn't see any on the plate.

In the local food market no one knew what aubergines and courgettes were. Lino started up restaurants in Preston, Lytham St Anne's, Bolton, Birmingham, the Trafford Centre,* Solihull, Leeds and other places. They were well-appointed, clean and comfortable, like the best places in Italy. Prices were moderate, in order to compete with the pubs. The aim was to offer an elegant and comfortable ambience all could afford, the kind of place Lino himself would have liked to go to when he went out. But not everyone approved. The locals preferred to go to the pub, with its smelly carpets and pints slopping with beer. Michele Pagliocca from Bari started about twenty successful eateries in Glasgow, but they're not Italian. He wouldn't dream of opening an Italian restaurant: "Where can I find the staff capable of cooking Italian food and the clientele capable of appreciating it?" Andrea Riva, of the Riva restaurant in Barnes, who has thought long and hard about these questions, agrees: "Italian cooking has always had to make compromises and adapt its dishes to suit British tastes." In the 1960s, the first Italian owners of popular restaurants were Mario Cassandro and Franco Lagattolla, who ran the trattoria La Terrazza, in Soho. Neither of them had a professional background in cooking in Italy; Franco had been born and educated in England. In a short period they opened a chain of restaurants, which became a company quoted on the Stock Exchange and was eventually sold on. They created a famous dish known as "chicken breast *sorpresa*", a dish which required a lot of butter, oil, breadcrumbs and egg for the coating. "In Italy, a good chicken doesn't need any special cooking, just some rosemary and sage," says Rina Bosi, an Italian housewife. Doriano Castellani, of Lugana restaurant in Kent, is of the unshakeable opinion that "the majority of my British customers just wouldn't be able to appreciate the extraordinary flavour of a real chicken fed on grain. They prefer factory-bred chicken, wrapped in a slice of ham and cooked in the oven like that – so the chicken and the ham are both spoiled." Nicola La Verghetta* too, the owner of La Rucola in Little Chalfont, admits that the restaurants owned by the brothers Otello and Elio Scipioni, who were among the pioneers in opening up Italian trattorie from the late '50s onwards,* made adjustments for their clients' tastes, with menus which combined Italian, French and British elements, as well as some inventions of their own.

In the UK, the Italian terms "trattoria", "osteria" and "locanda" have lost their original meanings. In Italy they indicated unpretentious local establishments, often family-owned, frequented by a clientele who, like lorry drivers, for example, couldn't eat at home because of their work. The menus consisted of a few first and second courses and side dishes. The wine was limited to a choice of house white or red, of modest quality, served in carafes. The ambience was sober and functional – no special interior design in these places. Behind the informality of the service often lay a lack of professionalism. But in Britain, Italians, misled by their nostalgic memories, have used terms like "trattoria" and "osteria" for places that have menus suitable for British clients and where people go to dine out and to be entertained. For the British, going to a restaurant is an evening out, like going to the cinema or theatre. As well as providing the usual services, the staff in an Italian restaurant were prepared to play a role, the stereotype of the carefree Italian.

> *"For Italians the "piazza" is an important part of the culture. It's a place where people communicate with each other by having a cup of coffee or glass of wine together. Italian restaurants in the UK have taken on the role of the piazza, a place where you get to know other people and others get to know you."*
> (Enzo Cassini)

In this sense, the winning formula for Italian success has been the behaviour of the staff who serve the tables – their humility, friendliness, loyalty and good nature.* The quality of the food was of secondary importance, at least at the beginning. It was only because of the waiters' beguiling ways that Italian cooking in the UK came to be appreciated. Experience shows us that our palates need to be trained if they are to accept and appreciate new tastes. It was the power of persuasion of the people serving up the dishes which has made all the difference. British diners expect waiters to be courteous, but also entertaining, sunny and cheerful. "It's the Italian sun," explains Pierluigi Bianchi. "Most people are energized by it. With some people it goes to their heads." Ermanno Taverna,* a connoisseur and doyen of the Italian restaurant trade, used to say: "We pay compliments to all the women – the pretty ones because they charm us, and the plain ones because it charms them," and he stressed the importance of the table service: "Our job is making people happy."

> *"I would recommend the experience of working as a waiter for at least a year to every young person, in preference to military service. It helps you to understand people through humility. Through attention to the needs of others, it teaches you how to become a gentleman."* (Pasquale Sarpi)

Walter Mariti, owner of the Pontevecchio restaurant in Chelsea, adds how Italian restaurateurs were the first to welcome children into their restaurants: "The British never brought their children when they dined out, because they were too noisy." Reflecting on his long experience of the profession, Lorenzo Berni says that "the Italians who started up restaurants from the 1950s to the 1970s brought soul and real love and passion to the business – even kissing, which was unheard of. We'd give a hug of welcome to customers when they arrived – quite unexpected for British people, who didn't allow such displays of emotion even among close family members. We satisfied a market need which the French, Chinese and Indian restaurants of the time didn't cater for."

And here are Gianni Segatta's thoughts on the Italian restaurant business in the UK: "The revolution in the concept of the Italian trattoria was marked by the opening of Mario and Franco's La Terrazza, redesigned with a welcoming atmosphere in 1960 by Enzo Apicella, who had suggested renewing the interior to the two partners. There were professional Italian waiters, courteous and welcoming, who were able to converse with the clients as well as serve them efficiently. Most British people hadn't experienced such a cordial atmosphere. As a result, Italian restaurants and trattorie began to multiply in Soho. The Chinese restaurant Mr Chow* also decided to employ only Italian waiters. In 1978, the opening of Cecconi's marked a second revolution in the restaurant trade: excellent chefs, impeccable service and high prices."

"The Chinese are good at cooking, but have you ever seen how they wait at table?" (Giorgio Casadei)*

The restaurant trade at the end of the 1980s

"During my time working in hotels, I learnt what needs to be done and, above all, what you should never do. In a restaurant, I wanted simplicity and elegance, with two elements in particular: clients shouldn't feel oppressed by the decor, and it had to be full of light. I've never liked dark restaurants. You feel the darkness is concealing something, and when it's dark people tend to whisper." (Giuseppe Cipriani)*

"The interior design of a restaurant is more important than the quality of the food," says Daniele Dalle Mulle after fourteen years' experience of working with Lino Della Pesca, who always stressed how important it was to keep the toilets clean and attractive. Dalle Mulle explains: "The design of a restaurant, the way it looks, is the first thing a customer sees, and it creates expectations. If the food and the service don't live up to those expectations, then the customer won't return." In the early 1960s, the cartoonist Enzo Apicella did the interior design for both La Terrazza in Soho and Tiberio in Mayfair,* emphasizing freshness, light and cleanliness. La Terrazza, as designed by Apicella – who by now was a successful designer and a figurehead for the new generation of restaurateurs, such as Alvaro Maccioni and Walter Mariti*

43

– became an influential model. But despite this trend, a large number of Italian restaurants in the UK at the end of the 1980s stayed resolutely behind the times and looked as they'd always done: smelly carpets on the floor, Chianti bottles used as candleholders, plaited ribbons of garlic bulbs and not much illumination. The waiters wore black jackets, often a bit the worse for wear, and bow-ties. The menus were only vaguely Italian, with invented dishes combining different international elements and with the frequent use of creamy sauces: *scampi pizzaiola* or *à la provençale*, steak Diane or "*boscaiola*", tournedos Rossini. The pasta and risotto dishes, all pre-cooked, used to swim in sauce. Any Italian customers were always advised to choose prudently and opt for a grilled steak cooked rare. Towards the end of the 1980s and the beginning of the '90s, some restaurant owners started to offer more regional cooking, paying more attention to the quality of the individual ingredients of dishes and respecting traditional techniques used in creating them. New chefs continued to arrive from Italy, and thus maintained the link with native inspiration. Some newspapers in Britain, especially the *Evening Standard* and its restaurant critic Fay Maschler, wrote articles praising the new trend and calling it "New Wave Italian".* In 1991 Gualtiero Marchesi brought his style of cooking to the Halkin Hotel in the heart of prosperous Belgravia. Jonathan Meades wrote a scathing and biased review in *The Sunday Times*. The wine promoter Niloofar Gardner has suggested that many restaurant critics pass their judgements only to reflect well on themselves: "They exalt themselves by rubbishing the others." Marchesi left London shortly afterwards, but the new approach he'd brought to cooking opened up new possibilities for Italian cuisine. All the new restaurateurs started to offer Prosecco as part of their wine lists, and the wine started to become noted.

Andrea Riva says that "the British don't want to eat Italian food which has been influenced by French or Japanese cuisine". In his view, the market for Prosecco in the UK is closely connected to the rise of the "New Wave Italian", which came to the UK from New York and Los Angeles, where it had originated, since the British are reluctant to accept innovations that come straight from Italy: "New trends tend to come via the USA." Riva's view is confirmed by the negative experience of some Italian restaurateurs, who in the early 1980s tried putting traditional regional Italian dishes on their menus, only to meet with customer indifference. "It was the style of cuisine which came filtered via the River Café and Orso – restaurants that had ties with the US – which initiated a new understanding of Italian food."

Two types of restaurateurs

There are two distinct categories of restaurateur. The first kind are stubborn and determined: they know exactly what they want and pursue it tenaciously; they're prepared to swim against the tide. Their courage sometimes pays off, but often makes it difficult for them to fulfil their aims. "They're determined to think for themselves; it's just how they're made," says Leonardo Di Canto,* talking of his favourite restaurant in Edinburgh, which struggled to stay afloat. Lucio Altana, of Lucio restaurant in Chelsea, tells how he once ordered a few crates of a famous Italian *cru*, the red wine Sassicaia, from a wine supplier. The distributor demanded, as a condition of the purchase, that he also ordered some Chianti from another firm, so Lucio told him: "I don't want the Chianti – but that's OK: I'll just take the Sassicaia off our wine list." The distributor called him back to apologize and offered him the wine without any conditions. Restaurateurs as determined as Lucio are good at introducing new products and at creating new fashions. We'll come back to this type of restaurateur, because they were the first to introduce Prosecco.

But the second kind of restaurateur, who follow the market or adapt their thinking to the circumstances they find themselves in, have a much easier task. They respond specifically to their clients' needs. The proprietors are entrepreneurs and are seldom if ever seen in their restaurants. The kind of restaurants they own are often near hotels or form part of a hotel, and are mainly patronized by businessmen who like the table service to be discreet. In the UK there are many restaurant chains which fall into this category. Yet the idea of several restaurants belonging to one person goes against the typical features of an Italian restaurant. Italian diners are demanding: they want special treatment, while the British are more disciplined and, in the words of Gino Taddei, "tend to follow fashions and trends". Italians are in fact more suited to the role of restaurateur than to the role of a diner.

Italians identify the restaurants they frequent by referring to the owner: you go to Tino's, or Mario's, or Toni's. They need to feel a direct relationship with someone, who becomes a kind of psychologist thanks to the dozens of people he meets every day and the variety of information on all sorts of matters he absorbs. In Italy, good restaurateurs, with a few exceptions, have a single restaurant. Mario Molino,* the first pizza chef to work with Pizza Express, complained that he never succeeded in setting up a chain of pizzerias with Italian partners: "We're just too bloody-minded." Restaurant chains are the result of American influence.

Names of restaurants

"The variety of restaurant names often reflects a native place or the roots of an identity you want to hold on to." (Sandra Griggio)

There was a time when Italian restaurateurs named their restaurants after famous cities, so you had Venezia, Roma, Sorrento, Lucca, La Spezia, Genova, Siena, Milano, etc., or tourist spots, like Capri, Ischia, Ravello, Portofino, and so on. Often adjectives went with the names of cities – Bella Napoli, Piccola Venezia, etc. – while some evoked the different seas round Italy – Adriatico, Tirreno, Mediterraneo – or famous Italian films: La Dolce Vita, Amarcord, Il Padrino, Amici Miei, Il Postino. Then the names of well-known artists and writers came into vogue: Leonardo, Da Vinci,

Caravaggio, Michelangelo, Dante, Ariosto, etc. – along with historical buildings (Colosseo, Arena, Trevi), traditional dishes (Bella Pasta, Metropizza, Pasta e Pizza, Maccheroni, Spaghetti, La Pappardella, La Carbonara) or popular wines and liqueurs (Frascati, Chianti, Barolo, Prosecco, Amarone, Limoncello, Sambuca, Strega, Amaretto). But restaurants were often named after their owners too – Massimo, Luigi's, Franco's, Mario's – or the saints after whom the owners had been named – Sant'Antonio, San Lorenzo, San Domenico, San Vincenzo, San Carlo, San Marco. References to the family are frequent, with Mamma taking pride of place of course: Mamma, Mamma Mia, Bella Mamma, Mamma Roma, Cara Nonna, Zi' Teresa. Others prefer to evoke the property market: Villa D'Este, Villa Bianca, Villa Rosa, Casa Mamma, Casa Romana, Casa Mia, Casa Giovanni. The surnames of owners are also used – Cecconi, Santini, Riva, Sarti, Turi, Locatelli – as well as the names of ingredients – Rucola, Ruchetta, Origano, Alloro, Rosmarino, Zafferano, Melanzana, Zucchini, Pomodoro, Basilico – including some of the basic ones – Sale e Pepe, Aglio e Olio, Pane e Vino, Grano, Spiga. Names were frequently preceded by Trattoria, Locanda and Osteria. References to famous restaurants in Italy were also common: Rugantino, Cambio, La Bussola, Cipriani, La Dolada, Assunta Madre, Quattro Passi.

Non-Italian owners of Italian restaurants have taken their inspiration from different aspects of the bel paese. Ian Mustafa, a Cypriot by birth, lived in Italy for a time and he's given somewhat unexpected names to his two London restaurants: La Figa and Il Bordello.* Ninai and Andrew Zarach called their Italian restaurant in Chelsea "Manicomio" ("Madhouse"). There is even a restaurant called "Bunga Bunga" in Battersea.

The "tyres" guide

"Restaurant reviews in the newspapers and in restaurant guides are often unhelpful: those who read them are more interested in criticizing than in eating." (Andrea Riva)

It was Arrigo Cipriani who coined the Italianized term for the *Michelin Guide* – the "tyres guide". The guide has given his restaurant Harry's Bar in Venice two stars in the past. Arrigo remarked: "Readers of guides belong to a herd and want to be led by a shepherd."*

On one occasion, when the representatives of a prestigious French company visited his restaurant, Lorenzo Berni hung three Ferrari tyres right in front of the table where they were dining.

Many Italians agree that the largely French *Michelin Guide* is not suited to judging Italian cuisine.* Restaurants and trattorie which offer an informal type of cooking are penalized under the Michelin system. Enzo Cassini, who was general manager of Michelin-starred restaurant Zafferano, nonetheless has said: "Even though I've spent many years working in France, where I encountered great professionalism in the sector, I don't think Italian restaurateurs should be influenced by the *Michelin Guide* judgements. The *Michelin Guide* isn't capable of understanding our culinary tradition." He also writes: "I'm at Courchevel at the moment, where there are four Michelin-starred restaurants, all of them half empty. Even the French elite have no more time for this fad – it no longer appeals." Today Enzo is busy introducing Italian cuisine in the restaurants belonging to Aman Resorts, a leading global chain of twenty-eight hotels. The owner of Aman, Vladislav Doronin, told him explicitly he "wanted 'mamma e papà' food" and asked Enzo to help.

Vices

City life changes the ways of living and thinking of the people who come from the countryside. Native Americans declared that "the concentration of peoples is the mother of all evils, both moral and physical... just like the loss of spiritual power which inevitably accompanies too much frequentation of your fellow human beings".* In the same way, deviant behaviour is a manifestation of city life and can be found among restaurant workers in the big cities. The most common vices are gambling, drugs and sex. At their worst, they become a form of slavery, so it's paradoxical that they're found in people who, in their desire to wander around the world, have chosen to uproot themselves from their own countries as an expression of their own autonomy.

The use of drugs is common. Paolo Recina, of the Portofino restaurant in Worcestershire, has remarked: "The use of drugs can often be found among those who work in the restaurant trade; the work is stressful, and sniffing cocaine can give you the stimulus to continue and takes tiredness away." Chefs are like artists: drugs and alcohol might increase their misery, but they also, at the same time, help them to become more creative.* Someone once said that "Artists find reality intolerable". Healthy individuals, when they get tired, have a good long sleep, but there are some people who aren't looking for harmonious living. They want to find ways of suffering so that they can become more productive. "It's above all the second-rate who are prepared to use any means whatsoever to try to become first-class," a leading chef has declared, referring to some of his colleagues. Drug abuse also creates economic dependency, and hence the need to increase the money coming in. A food supplier for London hotels succeeded in selling to all the head chefs – French, Swiss and other nationalities – by offering them a bribe that corresponded to a percentage of the value of the food they bought. After a detailed investigation, the British tax authorities discovered what was going on; the supplier had to pay a hefty fine and close down his business.

Angelo Pigatto has given us this description of a victim of cocaine use: "A couple of years ago I bumped into Antonio. We'd known each other for years, since we grew up in the same small town, but I hadn't seen him for a very long time. I was taken aback to find him, middle-aged like me, looking really run-down, riding a bike and wearing a pair of creased trousers and with a rucksack on his back. He'd left for England in the 1980s and built up a small chain of restaurants. He drove around in a Porsche and was always surrounded by beautiful women. For the rest of us, twenty-year-old penniless students, Antonio was a kind of legend. So I asked him what on earth had happened, and realized my question had come at the right time – he wanted to talk and tell someone about his life: 'I've just come out of rehabilitation. I tried AA, but I just couldn't keep it up. But the real problem was cocaine. I began taking it when I owned several restaurants, and life was great. To keep going – the long working hours, the important business meetings – I started to sniff cocaine. At the beginning the effect was fantastic – I didn't put a foot wrong – on the contrary, I did everything much better. I felt really alert, I never got tired, I felt confident and full of élan – all my former shyness vanished. As time went by, I needed to increase the doses to maintain the same effects – and so it went on, slowly but inexorably. I got to the point when I had to sniff just to get out of bed in the morning. Now I've lost everything, I don't have a job, I've got huge debts with the banks and my friends. I do a few odd jobs here and there from time to time.' It was obvious from looking at him: cocaine had ruined his life, after it made him think it was improving it."

"Chefs are magnets for women. The smell of garlic and sweat attracts them. It's lucky my wife has always been by my side, watching me like a hawk." (Franco Taruschio)

Italian emigrants in the UK didn't have any difficulty in starting relationships – or, put more bluntly, in having sexual relationships with the opposite sex, in contrast to the complex etiquette of courtship which was the norm back in the Italy they had left. In the restaurant world there's a common image of women as sexually available. Once, during a heated discussion on the matter which took place in the Giuliano restaurant in Edinburgh, someone came up with the priceless assertion that "all women are hookers, except for my mother", to which a waitress replied: "women must make do with the men they find today." Restaurant staff are courteous and flattering towards customers: they know when women clients are in need of kindness and understanding, and after a couple of glasses of wine they're ready to talk. For an unmarried man who enjoys affairs with women, this wouldn't be a problem; it becomes one when there's a family to look after. Then the man has to keep things concealed, make sure he never lets on, manage his time to keep them all happy. It's normal for Italian men, coming as they do from a Catholic country, to confess their exploits to their male friends, sometimes in excruciating detail. But adventures can be risky. A mutual liking between a man and a woman can evolve and start to demand both emotional and financial commitment. Enrico Proietti, of the restaurant Baraonda in Manhattan, takes a rather advanced view in his belief that "infidelities are like salt – they spice up a marriage", but other episodes in the Italian restaurant world in the UK suggest that this attitude isn't really workable. The end result is often family breakdown, neglected children and falling standards at work. "There are lots of stories on this subject – more interesting than those to do with Prosecco," Egidio Marino, of Gi Trattoria in West Wickham, jokingly said. He knew of someone, for example, who'd managed to get two women pregnant at the same time. Enzo Cassini is convinced that "men and women aren't made to live together", and perhaps that's also true in the restaurant world.

"Behave yourself, and if you can't behave yourself, be careful!"

There's a well-known case of a restaurateur, married to a beautiful and upstanding wife, who used his restaurant in order to satisfy his sexual and emotional appetites: he'd employ pretty waitresses who came to him from a catering agency. With fatherly attentions, he won their trust by offering them trips and dinners; in his predatoriness he had no moral scruples at all, and even pursued the daughters and wives of his friends. The earnings from the restaurant were not enough to satisfy his lifestyle, so he started to delay paying his suppliers. Then he began to chop and change the legal status of the business in order to hoodwink both his friends and the tax authorities. Now he's faced with suppliers demanding payment, not much business, a naive wife and waitresses who never stay for more than a few months at most.

"But our women clients are also difficult," maintains Luciano Beccarelli, who, with his business partner Sergio Dellanzo, managed the Val Taro restaurant near Piccadilly Circus. "When I pretended to be the good-for-nothing male, with two failed marriages behind me and three neglected children, women were always gentle and generous with me. Then I told them the truth: I'm a serious person, I'm still living with my mother, Pierina, and I'm looking for a lasting relationship. Then they'd tell me I needed a psychiatrist, not a woman, and upped and left."

Relationships with women – whether as wives or mistresses – can often affect, quite seriously, the independence and initiative of a businessman. On occasion even real misers can become transformed, splashing money out in the company of their lovers. Legal separations can become financially damaging for wealthy businessmen. British law tends to protect the women in such cases – and rightly so – but often doesn't draw a distinction between those who are genuinely entitled and the gold-diggers. "My divorce cost me almost as much as Prince Charles had to pay for his," complained Peter Rosignoli of the Poissonerie de l'Avenue, thinking of the hundreds of thousands of pounds he had to pay out on legal fees and the millions he had to give his ex-wife. Several men have made serial marriages, each one ending in the same problems, as if experience taught them nothing. Some women are very accepting – one example is the English wife of a Tuscan restaurateur, who agreed to look after the little daughter of an extramarital liaison he'd had with a Thai woman, while he went off to live in Bangkok.

"You find those who solve problems and those who just create difficulties for themselves," says Luigi Colazzo of La Pappardella restaurant on Brompton Road. When he arrived in the UK, Luigi was immediately alert to the dangers of gambling. He tells the story: "In the 1980s my brother Giorgio and I decided to go on a long holiday with two close friends. On the first day of the trip, on the boat across the Channel, our friends lost all their money in the casino on the ferry, and Giorgio and I had to support them for the rest of the trip." Many restaurateurs, addicted to gambling, manage the business of running a restaurant badly. When business is difficult, they blame the downturn on the economy – for them the economy is always on the way down. But some lose their profits continuously, because they gamble away their entire income; the most reckless soon find themselves without either a home or restaurant. Poker is a dangerous game for those who like to gamble. A restaurateur once went home after playing poker and asked his wife: "What would you do if you found yourself with a hand of four aces?" "I'd bet the house!" she replied instinctively. "That's what I was trying to tell you," he said. "We need to find somewhere to rent." The UK Government encourages the gambling industry,* but the flip side is that many weak-willed individuals have lost their hard-won earnings. Italians who escaped from conditions of poverty return to being poor, because gambling closes off all other prospects from its victims.

"Good customers are the ones I seek out: those who seek me out have usually got problems." (Pasquale Cannarile)

Individual vices always have to be seen in context. Some restaurateurs with these addictions don't manage to settle their bills and are forced to change suppliers of food and wine, and thus offer very bad opportunities for sellers working with new companies and new wines, such as Prosecco. As time goes by, this kind of client tends to be remembered fondly, as they were funny and always up to something worth talking about. But there's a price to pay, and sooner or later the bill comes along. Bankrupts are not always amusing for the people they owe money to. Stefano Flenghi, a distributor of Italian products in London, is frank: "I'm lucky in having the support of a wife and two fantastic kids behind me, otherwise I might have taken the law into my own hands with debtors and probably ended up in prison." Gambling aside, we must make a distinction between those restaurateurs who fail because they find themselves in genuine difficulties and the tricksters who profit shamelessly out of those who trust them. Some restaurateurs listen to the dishonourable advice of accountants and lawyers, and when there's a loophole in the law avoid taxes and paying suppliers in order to conceal illegal dealings, justifying their behaviour by saying they're following expert advice. The law cannot succeed in incriminating them, and this appears to relieve their conscience and hide the reality of what they do – which is that they are thieves, and a lot more dangerous than the ordinary kind.

Solidarity

The studies about Italian migration reveal the solidarity that existed among Italian migrants in the second half of the nineteenth century. They'd find jobs and then get their families and neighbours to emigrate and work for them (so-called "chain migration"). The phenomenon on occasion bordered on child exploitation, and there are several cases of dubious practices in bringing children over. A sum of money would be sent to the parents together with a return ticket – if the journey wasn't undertaken on foot – with a promise of food and lodging once they'd arrived. The employers, called "*padroni*", forced the children to become street traders; the unluckiest among them were made to beg in the streets. The history of immigration has its dark sides, even though their hard experiences taught many children the commercial skills needed for the period.

'The padroni *are cruel and pitiless masters, and treat the children just like slaves. If the little ones do not bring home a sufficient sum, they are cruelly beaten and ill-treated* [...] *and sent hungry to bed."* (W.H. Wilkins)*

"Italians tend to cheat each other, in contrast with other peoples, who live cooperatively within their ethnic group." This observation from the salesman Marco Olivieri is certainly true in some ways. The restaurateur Nicola La Verghetta puts it even more strongly: "Italians are jealous of each other – as a nation, we've the least sense of solidarity you can find." In the early 1970s, Enzo Bucciol started up an Italian restaurant in London, in the Shepherd's Bush area. The Italian staff he employed turned out to be unreliable and exploitative. The experience induced Enzo to switch to French cuisine and employ non-Italian staff. Giorgio Casadei recounts another episode, involving two business partners of a restaurant a stone's throw from Piccadilly Circus. "They'd had a disagreement. In the '70s the British tax authorities targeted one of the partners for avoiding tax on a large proportion of the restaurant's earnings. He was intending to invest the money back in Italy, in his home village of Borgotaro. The money was confiscated, and he was sent to prison for six months. Reliable sources of information point to the other partner as the person who informed the authorities."

But circumstances have altered over the course of time, and a truer sense of solidarity has begun to spread, even if it can still happen that those who have too much on their mind sometimes forget the favours they've received. Italians who live in poverty or find themselves in difficulties can be extraordinarily supportive of each other. In many cases, a poor person's wealth is the people who surround him. However, it's too easy to overlook this when you make money and forget the past and what you once were. The supplier Emilio Apicella has witnessed this transformation in an old friend: "Now he's wealthy, all he thinks about is money and how to save it. He's always preoccupied." But for Rinaldo Mollura it's different: "Now I've got some money behind me I can let myself relax. I feel more honest." Angelo Camassa declares, with the wisdom that comes from a career which has had its fair share of ups and downs: "When you're at the top and things are going gloriously, you become superficial; it's in difficult times that you rediscover your true humanity."

This is the most emotionally involving part of the story. The introduction of Prosecco and other Italian products into the UK market has created networks of collaboration and trust which exist quite apart from commercial considerations. An entire book would not suffice to relate the many important occasions on which the Italian community has shown its solidarity, but here, unbeknown to their protagonists, are some episodes which reveal this positive aspect, as well as how collaboration has often enabled people to overcome problems.

The custom of inviting fellow Italians from the same town or village to join you in the UK is still practised. Franco Papa of Florians has encouraged a twinning between his birthplace Palazzolo Acreide and Crouch End, where he lives and works. The inhabitants of Crouch End know Palazzolo Acreide and vice versa. Franco has helped people from his village to find work and settle down in the UK. He encourages mixed marriages.

Roby Gardetto, the owner of the Cambio restaurant in Guildford, used to offer free lunches to an Italian salesman who was just beginning his career. One day the man, embarrassed, insisted on paying the bill, but Roby told him: "You'll never need to pay when you come to eat here!" And for twenty years he's kept his word.

Franco Rimonti, a promoter of Italian products, didn't have to think twice about paying out five thousand pounds to help a friend in difficulty. The money was never repaid, even after a long time. Franco has often been through hard times, but his attitude has always been: "When you're all right with the world, just let things be and turn a blind eye."

Lorenzo Berni of the Osteria San Lorenzo would neglect the British Prime Minister if on the same night an Italian was among the diners ready to talk about squid, polenta and Prosecco.

Teo Catino of the Pagliaccio restaurant in Fulham has on several occasions lent money, sometimes large sums, to help friends in their business activities, knowing full well that he might never see the loans returned.

Ermanno Taverna offered his house in London to a family who'd been homeless for over six months. When the family arrived in the house, they found a bottle of champagne and a welcoming note. They managed to send cash in an envelope to him as a token of thanks, but Ermanno returned the envelope to the sender.

Carlo Cataldi of the Lizardo restaurant lent his delivery van for long periods of time to help a seller distribute cases of Prosecco, without asking for anything in exchange.

Umberto Scomparin,* who worked as a waiter in several Italian restaurants, died recently, leaving a wife and young children. Simon Piovesan of the Due Veneti restaurant and Angelo Cane of Vinum established a fund to which anyone who'd known Umberto could make a donation. The money collected in this way will be made available to his daughter, so she can pay her university fees.

As well as showing solidarity among themselves, the Italians in the UK also organize fundraising initiatives for good causes. Raffaele Gambardella and his business partner Paolo Fattore of the Villa Bianca in Frimley in Surrey organize an evening event every year in memory of the wife of their other business partner, Rino Testa, who passed away after a long illness. The proceeds from the evening, which also includes an auction, are given to a local hospice where their partner's wife ended her days.

The sommelier Giovanni D'Orsi tells the story of his Calabrian friend Salvatore Verardi, the manager of the two St Giles Hotels, one in London and one near Heathrow airport: "On Christmas Day Salvatore provided the turkeys, which he roasted himself, for the old people in two local care homes. It was his own idea, and done without any publicity." And since Salvatore himself has fallen ill, he has taken to raising money for the hospital where he's receiving treatment. He says: "At first I didn't give any thought to these things: one took the good things in life for granted. Now, at the end of every day, I thank the Lord for everything that's happened to me."

Wine consumption in the United Kingdom

The idea of introducing Prosecco into the UK would never have got off the ground had it not been for the Italian presence on the country's restaurant sector. Those working in the wine trade found it difficult to understand the British and their attitude to alcohol. During the 1980s in the Veneto, where people enjoy drinking, the problem of alcoholism manifested itself quite differently. There were solitary alcoholics who, starting in the morning, drank themselves silly in local bars before going back home in the late afternoon to sleep it off, while others occasionally got drunk but retained enough self-respect to feel sheepish about it afterwards. Families of agricultural labourers in the region would sometimes give a sip of wine to small children, while a fourteen-year-old boy, already working in the fields, would be allowed to drink a glass of wine with his meals. Wine at lunch and dinner was an integral part of the meal. But in Northern Europe, in Luigi Beccarelli's view, "the lack of sun means people drink more alcohol". Marco Cremonese, who lives in St Andrews in Scotland, has noted how, with the onset of winter and bad weather, sales of alcohol double. In the UK getting drunk is often a group experience, with young people and adults going out at the weekend on a self-destructive binge. In Italy a person getting drunk is seen humorously as a "donkey", a bit of a simpleton, but the English word "drunkard" suggests someone who's a danger to society. The phenomenon of alcoholism in the UK is a long-standing one, although television and the press wage a continual campaign against the dangers of drinking too much. Obviously the British aren't all like this – you need to go below the surface to know a population well and be better integrated to understand them. Yet there's always a risk that some foreigners see the UK through some of its pubs and can acquire the idea that the country is full of drunkards. This whole argument about alcohol consumption is clearly of great importance for serious wine producers and sellers who, precisely because of the value they place on their product and their involvement with it, are not aiming for this kind of consumer. The British Government imposes high taxes on alcohol in an attempt to limit excessive consumption;* year on year they're raised, penalizing moderate consumers. But while the tax on alcohol keeps going up, the number of alcoholics never diminishes.

In 1980s London, with its wealth and diverse population – which partly stemmed from foreign investment, especially Arab and Japanese – seemed an entirely different place from the rest of the country. Outside London there was less dynamism and fewer economic opportunities. Alcohol consumption was largely of beer. In the Midlands and the north of England, the population seemed to lack energy, taking refuge in ironic self-deprecation and confining expressions of national pride to sport. They looked to the Government for help with their problems, and the Government was inclined to demagogic pronouncements. In contrast, Germany was well-off, and its wealth was more evenly distributed. Cities like Hamburg, Cologne, Frankfurt and Munich offered good opportunities for the marketing of Italian wine. The Germans were hard, purposeful workers who spent their holidays on the Adriatic beaches in the Veneto and appreciated Italian food. Luciano Bazzani, one of the early promoters of Prosecco internationally, scored an almost immediate success with the product in Germany. But in the UK a not-indispensable product like Prosecco had very little interest for the poorer classes, who were in any case unaccustomed to drinking sparkling wine. For the well-off, on the other hand, wine consumption was seen as a privilege and a marker of both their economic means and cultivation. Prestigious French wines have always played a primary role in the UK market; the British like to bestow social cachet on certain wines, turning them into expensive symbols.

"'I love this wine,' a customer once remarked on buying a bottle in an Italian delicatessen. 'What word would you use for the person you love if you can say you love a bottle of wine?' the shop assistant asked him. He thought 'love' was an exaggerated word."
(A sales rep)

Francesco Bisetto, from Treviso, a cultivated man and a food connoisseur, says that the cost of a bottle of wine bears no relation to its real value once you start paying more than 100 euros. However, like the restaurant trade, wine production is a business; enthusiasm for producing wine is also enthusiasm for selling it on the market. The restaurateur Giuseppe Turi, who is a passionate connoisseur of wine, has invested his savings in vintage wines and expects to make a handsome profit on them. Why are some consumers prepared to spend thousands of pounds on a bottle of wine? The question is one even sommeliers find it hard to answer, even though they ask huge prices for vintage wines in the restaurants where they work. High prices, according to Virgilio Gennaro, the wine director of Locanda Locatelli in London, are caused by the scarcity of the product, together with its prestige and the demand for it. This makes sense from a commercial point of view. Roby Gardetto remembers his best customer, who liked to buy expensive wines. He was an Italian, a dealer in Ferraris. He wasn't a wine expert, so the famous name on the bottle and its high price were a way of reassuring him that he would cut a good figure with his guests. This view is backed up by Andrea Chiumiento, the Campanian manager of the Mediterraneo restaurant in Portobello: "In most cases, famous vintages are bought by people without knowledge of wine" – while Isa Bal, the head sommelier at the Fat Duck in Bray, Berkshire, openly admits that buying extremely expensive bottles of wine is mostly a form of exhibitionism on the part of wealthy customers. As Arrigo Cipriani puts it: '"Only down-at-heel aristocrats really understand food and wine, especially wine" – adding, apropos of the wine producer Angelo Gaja: "He never orders his wines in our restaurant – they cost too much!"* For the nouveaux riches or those with some money to burn, whose spending power outstrips their knowledge, it's important to show they know about wine, not in the sense that they know how to appreciate its qualities, but as an indication of their wealth. People with common sense cannot understand why others are prepared to pay such prices. There are exceptions. The footballer George Best, who liked to visit Italian restaurants and drank wine with ice cubes in it and couldn't tell the difference between Lambrusco and Barolo, admitted that he sometimes ordered vastly expensive wines just to see the waiter's face when he did so. A good waiter likes to provoke and tease his clients and challenge them. He has a kind of admiration for the prodigal diner who's happy to splash his money around and who'll supply the waiter with plenty of stories he can tell to outsiders who are unfamiliar with this kind of excess.

But almost everyone agrees: there's no such thing as intrinsic worth. The fashions of the market set up trends and habits. For those who dine on caviar and *foie gras* and those who eat burgers and fish and chips, some Italian dishes have carved out their own hard-won niche, such as a Caprese salad, which combines tomatoes, mozzarella and basil dressed with olive oil. This inspired the later successes in introducing Prosecco, which in the same way managed to create a space in the market for itself between the consumers of expensive French clarets and those whose preferred tipple when they drink wine is le Piat d'Or* or Liebfraumilch.

Luigi Marinelli, the former agent for the wholesale company Ciborio, confirms just how few Italian wines were available in the 1960s: "The most commonly found were white Lambrusco, a sweet Orvieto, Soave, Valpolicella, Chianti and Asti Spumante. Wine-drinkers knew their names, but the qualities of the wines from different producers escaped them. Every now and then a new wine would appear on the market, owing to the determined efforts of sellers and importers." So towards the end of the 1980s a typical wine list found in an Italian restaurant included, in addition to the wines listed by Marinelli, Barolo, Verdicchio, Frascati and Bardolino. Another popular wine was the Sicilian Corvo, made from the Nero d'Avola grape. Lambrusco and Asti Spumante started to decline in popularity. Chianti – in all its different versions – is produced in the countryside from which it takes its name, between Siena and Florence, and its enduring reputation can be attributed to its place of origin, since Tuscany has always been one of the areas in Italy most favoured by the British. When it first became known in the UK, its typical straw-wrapped bottles were a standard ornamental feature in Italian restaurants. There were many emigrants from Tuscany, and they certainly played their part in introducing Chianti into the UK, even though some people cast doubts, *sotto voce*, on their entrepreneurial skills: "Tuscans aren't as generous as people from the Veneto, or Campania, or the Abruzzo," is the view of Emilio Apicella, the former salesman for Mondial Wine, who comes from Salerno (Campania). Giorgio Casadei recalls the Tuscan wine producers who would accompany him on his selling trips: "None of them – counts, barons, marquises or peasants – ever paid their way. The bill for a meal would arrive, and they'd all excuse themselves to go to the toilets." But not all Tuscans are like this. Daniela Franchini, who works for Zonin UK and is herself from Florence, tends to agree but also draws distinctions: "You need to distinguish between the part of Tuscany closest to Liguria and the rest of the region. Tuscan successes are certainly down to our determination, but it's true we don't share the sense of sporting entrepreneurship you find in other parts of Italy." Frascati is associated with Rome. Lorenzo Berni recalls that "after the war, in the 1950s, Rome with its cinema and fashion industries was the most sophisticated Italian city. In that period Frascati was all the rage." In Britain there were restaurants called Frascati run by Italians who had fond memories of the Lazio region from which they came.

Again, the characteristic bottle with its smooth shiny glass and mesh covering helped its popularity. Enrico Toscani, the Roman owner of Sugo restaurant in Notting Hill Gate, describes its character as not "having any particular flavour. It's not difficult to like for those who aren't used to drinking wine. This is why Frascati was popular when wine consumption was just taking off in the UK. The British began with sweet wines like Asti or Orvieto and then went on to drink gentle or 'easy' wines like Soave and Frascati. Over time the palate gets trained, and then you can introduce dry wines with more distinctive 'noses'". A successful example of these was Pinot Grigio, thanks to the presence of good producers: Santa Margherita,* Pighin, Jermann, Marco Felluga, Livio Felluga and others. Among the reasons for its success was perhaps its name, which the British pronounce with an air of achievement. Year on year it has been the Italian white wine that has sold most bottles in the UK. The companies that pioneered Pinot Grigio are now lost among a proliferation of elaborately imaginative labels in which the producers are identified by an abbreviation. Giuseppe di Franco, who has worked for forty years as a salesman for Alivini* in London, predicts that Pinot Grigio will soon go the way of Asti and Lambrusco: "History repeats itself. New wines start off well, they become popular and then, as the quantity of labels increases and the quality declines, their success burns itself out." Daniele Dalle Mulle adds: "When an Italian wine is introduced, lots of producers and bottlers start to produce it in huge quantities, and consumers are faced with too many different qualities and prices." Gradually, though, Italian wines at higher prices started to appear on the UK market: Gavi di Gavi, Barbera d'Alba and Barbera d'Asti, Brunello di Montalcino and Amarone della Valpolicella. Sparkling or spumante wines from the areas around Franciacorta and from the Trentino were also available, but they didn't sell particularly well, since British consumers tended to regard Italian spumante wines as merely second-rate imitations of champagne. It was from the end of the 1980s onwards that various promoters from all the Italian regions really started to work to introduce the British public to the whole range of Italian wines in all their diversity, including – using a variety of methods – Prosecco.

PART TWO

Treviso – the happy province

Prosecco is the wine of Treviso – or at least in the past it was. Long ago, this area, right in the middle of the Veneto region, and known as the "Marca trevigiana" (the "March" or "Province" of Treviso, also called "Marca Gioiosa", "the happy province"), supplied agricultural products to the city of Venice. The Venetian nobility built country villas in the Veneto mainland, which also served as farms, growing crops and raising livestock. The decades which followed the end of the Second World War brought notable prosperity to the region. Artisans and small manufacturing firms flourished, a testimony to the inhabitants' capacity for hard work. But as well as daily work they also had time to practise a variety of sports and take part in other cultural events. They holidayed on the Adriatic beaches and went skiing on the slopes of Asiago, Enego and the Dolomites; cyclists rode the Pedemontana hills, while others paddled canoes down the rivers or snoozed on the lake shore waiting for the wind to come up for surfing. Just as importantly, the inhabitants of Treviso could not resist the artistic charms of Venice – the meeting place and melting pot of so many diversely talented people – and the melancholy bustle of its noisy narrow *calle*.

In such a dynamic atmosphere, their food and wine, the produce of their own region, became, to Trevisans, a synonym for their prosperity and well-being. Local restaurateurs started to put traditional dishes on their menus which used typical local produce, while at the same time experimenting with new culinary ideas of how to cook them.* Intellectuals like Beppe Maffioli and Giuseppe Mazzotti* played an active role in promoting the local cuisine as an expression of the local culture, an approach which contributed a lot to Treviso's reputation. The inhabitants of the city knew where each product came from and how good it was in relation to its provenance: a few kilometres could make all the difference in the taste and quality of the same crops, just like the endless variations in dialect which existed between one small place and another. In this context of innovation and creativity, two agricultural products in particular stood out: radicchio and Prosecco. Radicchio is a kind of chicory; sowing takes place in the late summer or early autumn. The old customary method of cultivation was, before the onset of winter, to tie the outer leaves up with string so that the inner leaves were protected, and then put all the harvested plants in heaps and cover them with earth and straw.* During the winter you took however much you needed to eat from the conserved pile and threw away the outer leaves, by now rotted away. What was left were the crunchy and bitter-tasting leaves at the centre. Although the methods of cultivation today differ from producer to producer, and people's eating habits have also changed, radicchio is still eaten on a daily basis and remains as good as ever. There are two common types of radicchio in the province of Treviso: the better known variety is the red Treviso radicchio, called "*tardivo*" or "*spadone*". It can be eaten raw, dressed with oil and vinegar, pepper and salt, but it's easy to cook. The other variety is the Castelfranco Veneto radicchio, also known as "*variegato*" or "*rosa che si mangia*"; this is normally eaten uncooked, and production is only for the local market. The story of Prosecco is quite different from that of radicchio: the growing interest in this sparkling wine, at first locally and then internationally, was driven by people who believed in the product and have worked to make it better known.

> "To the farmers of Treviso!
> ...If it is true that our province cannot as yet take its place among our fellow regions which are more advanced in wine production, you will find in the following pages fresh evidence of how your economic future is bright and as advantageous as our climate and our soil."
> (Angelo Vianello and Antonio Carpenè)*

The history of wine is an ancient one, but here we'll just give a summary of recent developments in the province of Treviso, based on the stories told by grandparents and parents. The Veneto region after the Second World War was largely rural; labourers would cultivate their small plots of land to satisfy the needs of their families. There was a stable with cows and oxen, a pigsty and chickens. Some people also had a donkey; a few could afford the luxury of a cart-horse for working in the fields. The main crops were wheat and maize. The pastureland was also used to plant vines; between the rows of vines there were mulberry trees, which in addition to supporting the vines were also used in silk production. The most common grape varieties were Clinto, Clinton, Americana Nera (Fragolino Rosso), Americana Bianca (Fragolino Bianco) and Bacò. The vines didn't require any special treatment: with Clinton you didn't even need to use scissors to cut the bunches of ripe grapes away. In the mid-1960s legislation prevented any commercialization of the wine that was produced, for muddled and often contradictory reasons. As a result, wine production of those grapes went into a decline and almost disappeared. Peasants planted new varieties of vine like Merlot and Cabernet on tiny plots of land. Tractors replaced oxen and donkeys. The family cellar was newly equipped with a wine-press, a vat for the pressed grapes, small barrels and demijohns for transport. During the grape harvest the work was hard. Harvesting the grapes, the pleasant smells of macerating, the sips of the sweet grape must and the light fruity wine which was the end result – these are the folkloric moments which are often recalled with nostalgia, at least by those whose only role was as spectators.* Rudimentary conservation and basic hygiene in the cellar meant the wine produced in this way never lasted long; after a few months it started to smell of fermented yeast. Whether it was good quality or rather less than that, the large bottle of red wine took pride of place at the table during meals. Alongside this domestic production, specialized winegrowers sprang up in the areas with named wines, in particular in the hills around Valdobbiadene and Conegliano, and the Asolani and Montello hills along the River Piave. The first school of enology was founded at Conegliano in 1876, and over the years it has played a vital role in the development of the sector. Vine varieties which became very popular included Marzemino, Verduzzo, Raboso, Refosco, Prosecco and Tocai. Local people would bring demijohns and fill up at the *cantine*, then bottling the wine to drink on special occasions such as feast days and anniversaries. As time went by, so the number and importance of specialized wine producers grew selling their wines to local bars and restaurants. This was the kind of context in which Prosecco started to come to the fore.

But the local and regional government lacked a long-term vision for the commercial possibilities of the agricultural products of the area – and even if one had existed, it would have been hard to get the locals to go along with it, such was their ingrained dislike of regulation and authority. There were no wine dealers, either in Italy or abroad, who were up to the task of making these wines something more than a mere food product. This was how most consumers treated it as well – a product like beans or onions: bricklayers would quench their thirst with a draught of white wine from a bottle with a flip top; the local drunks would drain a *quartin* – an extra-large wineglass – to keep the problems of the world at bay. However, population growth started to alter the economic character of the region; agriculture began to be replaced by industry and local manufacturing. Along with this, the role of the smallholder changed too: the vines scattered here and there throughout the countryside were dug up to make room for crops which demanded less effort to cultivate or for urban development. At the same time, under the influence of a rapidly expanding manufacturing industry, the wineries in the areas with named vines started to develop. They were no longer content to wait for customers to come to them to fill up their demijohns: they were driven by a new commercial impetus and started to promote their products on the national and international markets. Alessandro Marchesan* recalls that period: "My memories to do with Prosecco go back more than thirty years, to the Saturday mornings when my father Ottorino used to wake me early to join him on the annual trip he made to buy wine. The wine he bought wasn't just for the family, but for an entire village, including cousins, uncles, great-uncles and friends. We always made the journey in March – I remember it very well, since it was near to my birthday. I'd be wrapped up warmly, with gloves and a woollen beret, to face the last cold days of winter as they passed into the first mild, bright days of spring. The van was ready, packed with demijohns all neatly labelled with the names of the people they were intended for; it was like setting out on a voyage, with Dad at the helm, towards some happy destination. Just a short distance away we would stop to collect Uncle Marcello. He was short but strong – youthful-looking and always cheerful – smiling and talking at the top of his voice. I smile when I remember all the wise things he used to say, especially now I'm the same age as my father was then. Also, though the journey took less than an hour, it seemed a long way away. I remember how the landscape would change as we got nearer to the vineyards, still barely green at the foot of the mountains; gazing at the snowy peaks I could almost touch the silence. We would reach the family-run farm, in the heart of the territory producing Prosecco Superiore di Cartizze, where they would welcome us with salami and cheese, and bread just out of the oven, and glasses filled to the brim with straw-coloured wine. I'd be given a glass of Fanta orange-ade. The smiles on the faces of my father and uncle were really life-enhancing. Part of the trip involved going out to see the vines. We would meet a pair of winegrowers who proudly displayed their vineyards; today those fields are among the most expensive vineyards in Europe – and indeed the world. Then we would go back to the winery, where different wines would be tasted and the choice made of which Prosecco we'd fill the demijohns with to take home. My father and my uncle would concentrate on evaluating the wines – sipping, pondering, chatting and eventually deciding together as their faces started to flush. We loaded the van and drove home in triumph, because we were con- vinced we were carrying the best Prosecco you could find. Seated between my father and his trusted companion, I used to fantasize about the meal which would be prepared to go with the Prosecco – the perfect accompaniment, with its sparkling bubbles, to the warmth of the approaching summer evenings. My memories of Prosecco represent my first contact with the world of wine. They've gone with me all over the world and help me to rediscover the happiness of childhood. The sense of joy you feel in youth helps to chase away the moments of sadness and dismay. Prosecco is not just something to drink: it's a perfect glass of wine – simple, honest, straightforward and immediate – and you don't need a trained conoisseur's palate to appreciate it. It goes well with all kinds of food, even when you think it shouldn't. Wine-drinkers everywhere like it for its simplicity and freshness – to start and end the day, or indeed at any time."

A brief note on tiramisu

The district of Treviso has played a crucial role in the creation of the tiramisu and its diffusion throughout the world. The Treviso-born Dorino Sartor,* who at the beginning of the 1960s worked for the group of restaurants El Toulà,* recounts his own authoritative version of the events, which is quite different from the various stories and legends that have emerged over the years: "One of the traditions of the peasant families from the Veneto was grandmothers giving children a '*sbattutino*' – i.e. whisked egg in a bowl with sugar – with the words '*Dài, tirate su!*'

('Come on, take it up!'). Similarly, women who had just given birth were offered Marsala wine with lady's fingers by their friends and acquaintances, who would also say: '*Dài, tirate su!*' These popular traditions have merged to create the modern tiramisu, to which were subsequently added coffee, mascarpone and cocoa. Tiramisu does not originate from the restaurant industry, but rather from the collective traditions of the Veneto. As far as its development and diffusion are concerned, it is important to mention a number of restaurants in Treviso: Il Camin, Le Beccherie, El Toulà. The latter was actively responsible for its national and international dissemination. Back in the Sixties, I could never find this sweet in any restaurant outside the Treviso area."

Prosecco

"*Prosecco is made from a type of vine producing white grapes which has been cultivated for centuries only around Treviso. In recent decades it's become internationally famous, and as a result winegrowers in different countries have started to produce and sell it. This means that the brand must be protected against imitations and the other kinds of commercial exploitation which occur.*" (Dino Maule)

Since 2009, in order to protect its provenance, Prosecco has been used to define a geographical area. A village in

Friuli is called Prosecco, and the name is possibly connected with the wine. The authorities which decide in such matters have used the name to define the area of production; the type of vine used in the production has been given the name "Glera".* Prosecco is produced exclusively in the Veneto and in Friuli. The Carpenè Malvolti firm, which was founded in 1868 and was a leading producer of spumante wines, has promoted a national advertising campaign for many years. The founder of the firm, Antonio Carpenè, was an eminent scientist and as such contributed to advances in modern methods of wine production. Dozens of wineries have been set up, and more and more vineyards planted, while market demand has continued to increase. Here's Dino Maule's* summary of the commercial rise of Prosecco:

"It was around the 1970s that Prosecco started to gain in popularity, thanks to the efforts of the oldest and principal firm in the business, Carpenè Malvolti in Conegliano, Veneto. The following decades saw a significant increase in reputation and production, while the number of people involved in the business both in Italy and abroad also grew. Firms such as Valdo, Ruggeri, Bortolomiol, Nino Franco, Zardetto, Mionetto and others all took off during this period. The initial success of the Carpenè Malvolti Prosecco from Conegliano was followed by the fierce campaign waged by the producers of Valdobbiadene, who at first rivalled the older firm and then pulled ahead as market leader in terms of volume of production and reputation.

While Conegliano can boast that it started the trend, the Valdobbiadene producers can claim the prize for turning quality Prosecco into an international success story."

In contrast to the celebrated sparkling wines of France, Prosecco does not have the kind of historical tradition that the French customarily associate with quality wines. At the outset, official wine connoisseurs – especially those working for the media – underestimated Prosecco; some even criticized it. But as the market responded well, the experts came on board and supported its increasing popularity, which was due to firms and individuals working together with an energy that was in itself the expression of a successful time for the prosperous Veneto region. Prosecco is drunk young, while it's still fresh, and its effervescence sums up a happy and hard-working people. In Treviso and the surrounding area it's drunk at every hour of the day. For years it's been the habit to ask for it in a bar just like coffee or an ice cream. Drinking a glass of Prosecco in the morning adds brio to your day.

"For most consumers, drinking champagne is a form of marketing yourself." (Virgilio Gennaro)

Prosecco is to champagne as the Italians are to the French: two different ways of seeing life and the market. Champagne has a fascinating history and tradition, and the whole of France promotes it. It has a certain mystique, a special air that the French are past masters at giving to certain products. Drinking champagne is associated with partying and success; it's a necessary part of any celebration. It's an excellent sparkling wine without any doubt, but it goes beyond the quality of its production: it's become a symbol. Champagne is appreciated as an idea: you satisfy your mind when you sip a glass. In the past, astute producers managed to associate the drinking of champagne with the nobility and with royalty, and champagne has lived off the image ever since. Promotion of champagne focused on the emerging middle classes, who were looking for products which could epitomize their newly enhanced social status. The methods of production of champagne are more complicated than those for Prosecco.*

"French marketing is very good at creating a mystique around a product that enhances its value. Knowing too much about a product means you tend to value it exactly for what it is." (Attilio Mionetto)

Prosecco, by contrast, first became well known in Treviso and its surroundings. People found they liked it, and then very quickly it started to be drunk all over Italy. You can drink Prosecco on its own during the day and also with meals. It's a wine in the same way that mozzarella or parmigiano are classified as cheeses. It cannot be judged like other sparkling wines; its development has not been affected by the evaluations made by those who work in the trade. It's pointless to compare it to champagne;* it would be like asking whether sardines are better than oysters. It's the taste of Prosecco on drinkers' palates which has made it so successful; its success has been decided by ordinary folk who know what they like. Prosecco too has an ancient story behind it, but this was never used to market it, although now it's so successful people have become interested in its background. Some winegrowers would like to turn Prosecco into a kind of champagne, make its quality its chief selling point for an elite market, but, as Lorenzo Zonin has remarked, "The featherweight boxer can't expect to become heavyweight champion." Prosecco is an unpretentious sparkling wine, which most people like.

In the 1990s, Germano Marcato was the manager of the restaurant The Italian Touch, owned by Giancarlo Cioffi, in Cockfosters. He used to buy Prosecco from a farmer and bottled it personally using some empty bottles of Dom Pérignon which had been drunk by diners in the restaurant. During a dinner Germano offered three bottles of his Prosecco to a table with diners who didn't speak Italian. At the end of the evening, the diners, convinced they had drunk Dom Pérignon champagne, insisted on paying for the bottles, which they thought must have cost a fortune. But it's not as though they were naive: it's just that they had spent a very pleasant evening in the dimly lit restaurant, with music in the background, and hadn't had the time to reflect on the authenticity of the "champagne" they thought they'd been drinking.

Prosecco in the UK

Antonio Alfano, the son of Carmelo Alfano, of Ciborio,* tells the story of how his uncle Carlo once, back in the 1970s, took several restaurateurs on a visit to the province of Treviso. They played tennis and drank *ombrette*,* and he developed an enthusiasm for Prosecco. "Encouraged by the presence of the restaurateurs, he placed a very large order from a well-known wine producer. After a year, the Prosecco was still in the cellar; bottles of it would be given as gifts during the Christmas holidays."

At the end of the 1980s, Prosecco was unknown in the UK, and very few producers from Valdobbiadene and Conegliano had a presence in the UK market. Paolo Nolasco, a former partner in the wine-sellers Vinum, says that he cannot recall Prosecco being included in the catalogue: "For years it just wasn't a significant wine." Sandro Bottega,* the owner of the distillery and winery which is also named after him, travelled around the world when he was young, and could not understand why the British market was so difficult for Prosecco: "Why do I have problems with it in Britain, when I don't have them in Peru?"

At the beginning of the 1990s, one wine-producing firm with a little presence in the market was Gregoletto, which produced sparkling wines from Conegliano, distributed

by Alivini. The importers Winecellars* represented the
Carpenè Malvolti sparkling wines, but sales were limited to
a small number of clients. Prosecco from the Valdo winery
only made a rare appearance, just like the one produced
by Loredan Gasparini, imported by Enotria. When in 1994
Enotria acquired the distributor Winecellars, the owner,
Remo Nardone, showed no interest in continuing with
Carpenè Malvolti; he didn't think it was profitable to include
in the firm's list the oldest and most important of all the
producers of Prosecco. A youthful Gianluca Bisol, the owner
of a wine-producing company named Bisol, started to attend
wine fairs and showed more initiative than other producers
in trying to introduce his sparkling wines, including a still
Prosecco, to potential clients. Gianluca targeted the high-
end market, like the Italian spumante producers using the
"*metodo classico*", and initially collaborated with the food
distributor Danmar, owned by the Venetian Pietro Pesci.

The slow movement of Prosecco stocks caused problems
with its quality; it stayed refrigerated too long, and when it
reached the customer it was stale and oxidized. Small and
medium-sized producers had to wait for the role of the sommelier to emerge in the UK in order to begin to make their
mark; restaurateurs too started to realize the importance of
taking on well-informed staff. The number of sommeliers
has increased in the last two decades,* and this has meant a
much wider choice of wines becoming available. Sommeliers
are passionate about wine, sometimes against the interests
of their employers. Piero Quaradeghini of Etrusca Group

used to complain: "I don't run my restaurants as schools for learning about wine: they're supposed to be businesses." And Enzo Cassini remarks that "certain sommeliers are like rich spoilt women who go on a shopping spree with their husband's credit card. But it's also true that it's their efforts to increase customers' knowledge of a vast range of Italian wines that have led, decisively, to an improvement in the image of Italian quality."

> *"When you start to collaborate with a firm, you go in by the main door, and when you end the collaboration, that's how you should leave as well, not through the window."* (Dino Maule)

The Mionetto family

What the food writer Giampiero Rorato, from Treviso, has written on Prosecco is true: "Today's successes represent the fruits of a collective effort, which came about thanks to a happy combination of factors..."* Yet the achievement of the introduction of Prosecco into the UK must be attributed above all to the Mionetto family, who deserve closer attention.

During the 1980s, Mionetto in Valdobbiadene, producers of sparkling wines, was, in commercial terms, the most dynamic of the winemakers producing Prosecco. Dino Maule worked for them for four years as commercial director and remembers his time there vividly: "The Mionettos were an extraordinary family. I found myself working alongside the two brothers Giovanni and Sergio – the enologist – as well as their two nephews Attilio and Emilio, who'd been brought up by their mother Erilde after their father Francesco had died while they were still little. Two generations and four different personalities, doing different jobs in the firm. My arrival coincided with a golden age for Prosecco and the Mionetto family. It was pure luck. In racing terms, I arrived at Valdobbiadene when there was a thoroughbred ready to ride, rather than some old hack. From the mid-1980s onwards, the Mionettos were pursuing a notable expansion. In a very short space of time, sales were increasing year on year in double figures. The spread of the reputation of Prosecco was astonishingly swift. For consumers, Mionetto and Prosecco meant the same thing. After the phenomenal increase in sales in Italy, the decision was taken to focus on foreign markets, where contacts had up until then been limited to certain European operators in the sector, mostly German."

All four family members who formed the Mionetto firm were well disposed and good-natured. The courage with which they confronted difficult situations had a touch of genius mixed with madness in it. Attilio planned his strategy like a general: in his view, they needed an army of sellers to set out to conquer the international market.

In the 1980s, wine distributors in the UK showed no interest in Prosecco. There was no market for it, since the product was unknown. "When you're no one, only another no one is interested in you," Attilio complained. So, to combat the lack of interest, in 1988 Mionetto established a UK distribution branch called Le Tre Venezie and appointed the Venetian Giancarlo Fabbris as director, who was a former minority partner in the restaurant Cecconi's, and had been promoting Prosecco among his acquaintances and former colleagues,* with sales being limited to the bottles the owners bought to drink whenever they played cards. Under Fabbris's management, Giuseppe Lunardi was recruited; he'd come to England to join his girlfriend. Giuseppe managed to introduce Prosecco into Italian restaurants in North London.* He didn't speak English, so he enrolled in a school, where he made friends with the Irish principal; the two men enjoyed drinking grappa together. At that time, the sales of Prosecco to the school were higher than in any restaurants. After a year, Lunardi, disappointed by the prospect of only moderate earnings, decided to return to Bolzano, minus his girlfriend and with a knowledge of English limited to "Good morning" and "Good evening". His Irish friend, in the meantime, between glasses of Prosecco and grappa, had learnt to make a bit of conversation in Italian.

With the aim of selling the wine more widely, Le Tre Venezie sponsored Ciao Italia,* an association which included a large number of Italian restaurateurs, one of whom was stirred into action and offered to help. Ermanno Taverna, president of the association, recommended Prosecco to Tito Chiandetti, who was the buyer for the Forte Hotels group.

They ordered thirty pallets, and Mionetto shipped them out together with a vast amount of publicity material to support the promotion. Seventy-five per cent of the order was returned to Le Tre Venezie a year after the initial purchase. The hotels in the chain had included Prosecco in their wine lists, but the waiters had failed to get customers to try it.* The Mionetto family realized they couldn't rely on chance, and also that they needed to promote knowledge of the product. From then on, they sought out friends who were willing to help, restaurateurs who were keenly motivated, Italians who could think innovatively. They needed to find a new bottle that would help promoters to convince people to buy.* Mionetto suggested a bottle with a "string" design: a normal champagne bottle, but with a piece of string looped over the cork to hold it in place, a style of closure that probably originated at the beginning of the twentieth century. On the international market this visual feature stood out, since it recalled a link with the past. The string was applied by hand, and it suggested an artisanal rather than an industrially manufactured product, with rural overtones of simplicity. The sparkling wine, with a pressure below three atmospheres, an aroma of apples and an aftertaste of sugared almonds, pleased most of the tasters. The bottle of Prosecco with its loop of string* played something like the role the straw-covered Chianti bottle had once had, but the resemblance stopped there, since the Italian sparkling wine had nothing like the same level of sales in the UK market. The promotion of the "string" was helped by the original concept of decanting into a carafe placed in a transparent wine-cooler, which allowed the rising bubbles to be seen.* Indeed, Paolo Mancassola of the Valentino restaurant on the Edgware Road remembers that Prosecco in the beginning was bought to be poured into carafes.

After three years of activity, Mionetto closed the distributors Le Tre Venezie. It was in the red; the recession and the clients who had defaulted on payments meant it was unsustainable in a market that stubbornly refused to take off. Mionetto offered the distribution to the import company Enotria, founded by Remo Nardone in 1972. Sergio De Luca, buyer for Enotria, recounts his experiences of Prosecco and its introduction into the UK: "I was born in Vittorio Veneto, so I grew up surrounded by Prosecco. My grandparents were farmers; I'm proud to be the owner of a small vineyard of Glera vines and also to be a member, along with my family, of one of the cooperative wineries in the DOCG area. When I first arrived in England at the beginning of the 1980s, Italian wine was thought to be good enough for Italian restaurants, but definitely not comparable with French wines. I had a diploma from the school of enology in Conegliano, and I had some experience in the wine-import trade, so it was easy for me to find work. Towards the end of the 1980s, I went back home in order to find a local product, hoping to widen the range of wines that were imported into the UK. Remo Nardone, with characteristic foresight, sent me to reconnoitre the situation in Valdobbiadene, where a new producer of sparkling wines was revolutionizing the way Prosecco was sold. Mionetto used marketing strategies that were similar to those used by champagne producers. A close partnership between Enotria and Mionetto took shape. Our sellers, together with people from Mionetto, introduced Prosecco into the wine lists of the majority of the restaurants who were our clients, with the involvement of the owners, who became in their turn enthusiastic promoters of the wine. We shared the offices of Enotria in Park Royal; together we worked to spread the word about Prosecco, and the work we did was fundamental for its future success..."

Enotria* had about fifteen salespeople in their team; Nardone employed numerous youngsters who were brimming with enthusiasm, choosing only the best. Two brothers from the Romagna region, Remo and Giorgio Casadei, used to achieve the best results, entertaining clients with amusing jokes.* But the 1990s were economically difficult for the UK; one seller complained that because of the recession "I can't even sell to the clients who don't pay".

After the partnership had lasted two years, Mionetto and Enotria went their separate ways. Enotria had done a great job, and sales were steadily increasing, but Attilio liked to get on with things, and became impatient with what seemed to him too slow a rate of growth when it was compared with the Italian and German markets. Enotria stopped buying from Mionetto, and the wine producers turned instead to the distributors F&S.* The break between Enotria and Mionetto was the consequence of irreconcilable differences of objectives between the world of distribution and that of production.

There are, indeed, marked differences between the two sectors. Producers are tied to the cultivation of the vines and of the soil; they're often families who've been producing wine for generations. Their mentality is unlike that of modern businesses, which can change hands frequently. The farmer's attachment to the land cannot be measured with commercial criteria; he would only sell it if forced to; otherwise it's handed down to his children, who feel a family obligation to continue the work. The monetary value of a vineyard is far superior to the profits which can reasonably be expected to be made from producing wine. There are wealthy traders or industrialists who buy up vineyards for the prestige of it, just like owning a swanky car or a seaside villa. But for both the farmer and the investor, the returns are projected in the future. By contrast, the hard-working importer has to assess the demands of the market and choose the right products for it. Distributors don't have long-term programmes for the firms they represent: they need to make a profit quickly and sell whatever's in demand. These differences in outlook are often the cause of tensions between distributors and producers. The engaging Marco Olivieri, who worked as a salesman at the end of the 1990s, admitted he didn't know the names of the various Prosecco wines that were sold by the distribution company he worked for: "There were two thousand items in our catalogue – I couldn't remember the names of those we didn't sell much of."

*"The farmers of Valdobbiadene are the Arabs of wine.
They've struck oil."* (Sergio Mionetto)

Having acquired so much experience of the sector, in 1996
Mionetto decided to tackle the market head-on with new
and untested ideas and strategies. The firm sent out a team
of its own representatives who proposed Prosecco to small
importers and to restaurants that were in a position to buy
directly from the producer. Once a way was found to pay
customs duties, Mionetto moved rapidly. Under the new
scheme, the salesmen took on the role of go-betweens. In
London, involving the clients – i.e. the restaurateurs – more
closely meant that sales increased: most Italian restaurants
now included Prosecco in their wine lists. The task of
sounding out the territory outside London was entrusted
to Alessandro Allegretti, a native of Frosinone, the partner
and manager of a restaurant in Beckenham in Kent. With
his ready smile, Sandro knew immediately how to bring
people on board; he said: "I've never sold wine, but try
me and you'll see I'm successful." He took leave from his
restaurant and started off on his arduous campaign. He
left Kent, worked his way across East and West Sussex, and
then Hampshire and Dorset, before arriving in Devon and
getting as far as Cornwall. "It's a constant battle," he used
to say; he saw himself as a warrior. Then he headed north
on the conquest of Oxfordshire, Leicestershire, Yorkshire
– as far as the dry-stone-walled fields of Cumberland and
Northumberland. Here, after exemplary work sowing the

seeds, he halted, rather like the Emperor Hadrian. He focused above all on bringing small distributors and restaurateurs over to the cause of Prosecco. He included the cities of Manchester, Newcastle and Liverpool. In Scotland,* the distributor Quattro Stagioni run by Tony Turner was gradually increasing its activity, thanks to the efforts of Paolo Veneroni. Paolo was responsible for introducing various cocktails using Prosecco, including spritz, an aperitif made with Prosecco, a little water, some red vermouth and an olive or slice of lemon, or other variants. Inside the M25 there were seven sales reps carrying samples of Prosecco to all the potential clients in the Greater London area. Massimiliano Jacobacci,* from Rome, was especially well suited to dealing with the more prestigious clients, while the Calabrian (from Crotone) Gregorio Stabile* was active even at night, frequenting pizzerias and nightclubs. The Romanian Nicola Vescan focused on Turkish and Indian restaurants, while Leya Jet, a ball of energy from Singapore, covered Chinese restaurants. The Venetian Diana Ingram convinced Mr Bibiani, who was responsible for the catering in the House of Lords, to introduce Prosecco among the peers; the chamber became a regular client, with weekly orders. When Mr Bibiani retired, Prosecco was drunk at his leaving party. Roberto Simeone from Gaeta, an irascible southerner – and proud of it – grew to like Prosecco on account of his girlfriend Silvia, who was born in Valdobbiadene. He was the deputy general manager at PJ's in Covent Garden and once ordered twenty boxes of Prosecco without first consulting the owner, Owen Crinningan. Roberto was trying to explain to him why he'd bought the wine, when Owen silenced him by saying "shush" as you might to an annoying child. Roberto grew red in the face: "What did you just say?" His boss replied: "Shush." Roberto felt insulted, so stood up to Owen: "You're Irish and I'm Italian, so we've got something in common. If you tell me once more to 'shush', you won't even have time to dial 999!" In effect they were similar in character, and after a while found a way of getting on.

In February 1997 Mionetto organized a gala evening at the Caravaggio restaurant run by the Quaradeghini brothers. The theme of the evening was Treviso and its produce: Prosecco, radicchio, tiramisu, *fregolotta* – a typical tart found in the city – and *bibanesi*, short breadsticks made at Bibano by the entrepreneur Giuseppe Da Re. In the kitchen, good chefs such as Paolo Simioni, Alberico Penati and Stefano Cavallini produced inspired variations on radicchio and beans. The guests, representing over two hundred restaurants, were ecstatic, with some declaring they must visit Treviso. Sergio Mionetto, the enologist at the firm, was present at the dinner, complaining his hand hurt because he'd travelled over to the UK carrying a suitcase packed with twenty kilos of borlotti beans from Lamon, a village up in the mountains not far from Valdobbiadene. In his speech to the assembled guests, Sergio said how much he enjoyed being with country folk in the middle of vineyards; cities for him were a kind of prison. He hoped that everyone could understand how wine was all to do with the way we live and the earth we inhabit. A glass of Prosecco a day was enough to keep you in good spirits.* What Sergio knew about marketing techniques was fairly improvised; it was just as well his wife Solidea was there to restrain him. Every time he visited London to represent the firm, in every restaurant he visited he would go round the tables offering a bottle of Prosecco. He was once invited to the opening night of one of Aldo Zilli's restaurants, with lots of celebrities present; he put his finger in the other guests' glasses of Coca-Cola or champagne, obliging them to change glasses and choose Prosecco. A journalist from a national newspaper who was present reported: "There was a certain wine producer at the party, called Sergio, who was the most interesting figure there. He invited everyone to his house in a village with an unpronounceable name (Valdobbiadene). He didn't speak a word of English, but managed to communicate with his hands and eyes..." It was a sign of the times: a single individual challenging the big players who control consumption was winning acceptance. Mionetto's boldness was like a declaration of war and showed that Prosecco could make itself known and win a place in the international wine market. And when British visitors did come over, Sergio didn't take them to the prestigious restaurants of Venice, but to Toni Zanetton's vineyards and home, where for sixty years daily life had gone on unchanged. They were offered a piece of cheese accompanied by a bottle of Cartizze. Toni's wife, surrounded by farmyard animals, would churn the cream to make butter, while Sergio looked out for likely suitors among the guests as a potential husband for one of their daughters. The evening at the Caravaggio restaurant was an important publicity milestone in the growing familiarity with Prosecco and led to many importers including at least one Prosecco label among their wines.* Buoyed up with optimism, sales teams started to attract aspiring agents, such as Dante Diaferia, who set up a small warehouse in the City. Sales started to increase, with orders coming in from various retail sectors, especially the fashion industry, such as Moschino, Donna Karan, Ermenegildo Zegna and Vivienne Westwood. Terence Renati, whose hairdressing salon was on the King's Road, ordered a pallet directly from Italy and would offer his clients, as they waited for their appointments, either an espresso coffee or a glass of Prosecco. Gino Amasanti, the general manager of Costa Coffee, wanted Prosecco to be served at all the company's corporate meetings and functions.

The Prosecco producer Antonio Dal Bello once asked a business consultant what he needed to do to grow his company. The consultant replied: "First of all you yourself need to grow." To which Antonio replied: "The only way I can grow at my age is to start wearing heels..."

In 1999 the Mionetto family sold 40% of the company, for various reasons. They needed more money to invest in various projects, while a strict credit check on clients who owed money was needed. Attilio stepped down from managing the company. "The new guys are more capable," he declared as if he believed it; in his heart he knew the fun was over. Emilio said: "We've always been good-natured as a family, but we never stopped quarrelling. The newcomers work well together – it's a pleasure to watch them." But this conflict of ideas produced originality and innovation, while harmony and lack of imagination meant a shortage of new ideas. The new partners, inexperienced in the wine trade and only focused on short-term profit, didn't share the Mionetto family's vision for the company. "We just thought that everything that was old-fashioned was wrong," the new export manager, Marcello Gobbi, later confessed. The new management maintained the structure of the US market, where sales continued to increase, thanks to Enore Ceola, but in the UK Mionetto called a halt to the aggressive and resource-hungry marketing strategy, since the new co-owners had other ideas in mind. A new importer was chosen, Moreno Wines, which acquired exclusive rights to the sale of Mionetto products; after a short time, this decision led to a loss of Mionetto's leading position in the UK market. Other producers arrived to fill the gap, some of whom imitated the bottle with the loop of string in response to the market request for this.

Uncle Giovanni sold his share of the company in order to enjoy a comfortable retirement.* Attilio had no sympathy

with the bean-counters now at the helm and foresaw that
his vision for the company was destined to fade; after
a year he too, very reluctantly, decided to sell his share
and leave. The day of his departure was unmarked by
any celebration of the contribution of this man, who,
together with the rest of his family, had revolutionized
the market for Prosecco.* No thanks were forthcoming
for someone who had devised a military strategy for
increasing sales using an approach that was based on
respect for others and enhancement of their capacities,
who fought shy of easy solutions, whose words always
made you smile but also think, a real gentleman who
at the end of a meal would get up from his chair only
after his guests had got up from theirs.* He wanted to
see executives who were like philosophers and sales reps
who were like artists; seeing the family firm end up in the
hands of unimaginative number-crunchers pained him.
Stefano Cadamuro* remembers that someone once tried
to cheer him up by telling him: "Attilio, one day they'll
make a statue of you and put it in the main square
of Valdobbiadene"* – to which he replied, in dialect:
"Well, for that matter, they've already chiselled away at
my arse!"* After Attilio resigned,* Emilio and Sergio also
left the firm. Emilio, cheerful in both victory and defeat,
set up Col Saliz, producing Prosecco in the region of
Refrontolo. In retirement Sergio continued to pour his
heart and soul into working in the vineyards alongside
the labourers in Valdobbiadene. He produces Alma Forte,

his own Prosecco, with his date of birth, 18/06/38, on the label. When he offers a glass to his friends, he looks them in the eye and tells them to be careful how they drink: "I'm in that wine!" With the Mionetto family gone, the new owners' objectives changed, and the sales strategy focused on the easiest market for a leading company: the supermarket chains.

"The Mionetto family tried to create a festive atmosphere in the outlets where their Prosecco was sold. Their originality – which went counter to the prevailing trends – was to try to give Prosecco an air of informality, since they knew it was not just any ordinary wine." (Alessandro Maschio)

One project which had attracted the new partners into the Mionetto firm was the idea of establishing "Proseccherie", wine bars specializing in Prosecco. It was the culmination of the Mionetto family's vision: to apply their ethos and marketing ideas to the diffusion of Prosecco. No one in the history of the wine trade, except perhaps for champagne, had ever thought of setting up a place called "Chardonneria" with the aim of selling the most successful white grape in the world, or "Pinoteria", after the extraordinary levels of sales Pinot Grigio enjoyed in the UK. The Mionetto family's intuition was important: Prosecco could take its place alongside other Italian products which had become internationally famous, such as pizza, bruschetta and coffee, which had all given rise to places specializing in selling them. So "La Proseccheria Mionetto" was born, a wine bar where you could also eat simple traditional dishes, like a bar in Italy, serving quick, easily prepared quality food and drink. The bars were brightly decorated and lively; the idea was to make them welcoming and informal. The concept was inspired by franchises in the textile trade; as an initiative, it was part of the overall strategy of creating autonomy for wine producers outside the restaurant business, which was difficult to manage. The original intention was, after a trial run, to open Proseccherie all over the world. In the UK, the new partners in Mionetto accelerated the process, opening the first bar on the King's Road and a second one in Beauchamp Place, a stone's throw from Harrods. But neither worked out, and within a year both closed down. The project needed a large amount of investment, which the new partners were able to provide; what they were lacking was the determination and the courage to pursue ambitious ideas. So the Proseccherie idea was short-lived, but it did provide further publicity for Prosecco.

In 2010 Mionetto was sold again to Henkell & Co, a German production and distribution company.

Selling Prosecco

"There isn't a school for selling. Psychological skills, honed through long daily experience of meeting people, are what makes a good sales rep. You succeed in selling if you're on the same wavelength as the purchaser. I spend days and nights with my clients getting to understand them; we have a glass of wine together, and that way I get to know them thoroughly." (Marco Cremonese)*

Sales reps get good results if they listen to their clients. Gary Ison, who trains sales reps, declares that "the good ones listen 80% of the time and talk for the remaining 20%". Detailed praise of the product you're trying to sell is not always the best way to go about it: too often it's like parents praising their children; you start to wonder about bias. This is how the sales rep Giovanni Morabito explains his excellent results: "When someone asks me what makes for a good sales rep, I'm always stumped for an answer. For me it's like this: my work consists of turning up to appointments on time, well dressed (for the first meeting at least), and introducing the company whose products I'm selling. There's no philosophy or poetry about the matter. I propose the products that seem most suited to the type of restaurant I'm dealing with and try to be competitive but without compromising on quality. I don't get stressed, and I don't stress others. A ready smile helps a client to make a move. I've been a sales rep for six years, and I'm still a beginner compared to other colleagues who've been working for decades..."

At the end of the 1980s, it was difficult for Prosecco producers to recruit professional sales reps, since they didn't want to spend time on something which might not turn a profit. Companies that brought out new products attracted aspiring sales reps and focused on the link between the product and where it was produced. Speaking about the importance of the consumers, the sommelier Dino Bisaccia has declared that "winegrowers make efforts to win the liking of their clients, especially the clients who are going to be directly involved in promoting their wines, like sommeliers; they organize visits to the vineyards and the wineries where their wines are produced".

Wine reps love social interaction with smiling interlocutors and having a nice drink together during tastings. Gino Ruocco, one of the first sales reps to specialize in promoting little-known wines, used to say: "No one gets rich selling wine, but we have a good time." Giuseppe Di Franco adds: "There's always a reason to drink — either because you're sad or because you're happy." The early sales reps for Prosecco focused on the wine's cultural background and context: the Veneto region with its beautiful landscapes and architectural treasures, the hard-working people and the associated cuisine. Good sales reps inspire affection both for themselves and for the product they're selling. A group of affectionate and supportive consumers grew up round the marketing of Prosecco, and they were a determining factor in the growth of its popularity. At the beginning these collaborators were inexperienced, but tenacious and spirited; they were different from mercenary businesspeople: they were willing to spend time singing the praises of Prosecco to clients, without an immediate positive result that would match their efforts.

Two types of sales reps

"It's helpful for a good sales rep to understand marketing, but no one can work in marketing without experience as a sales rep." (Remo Nardone)

"I'm not the one who creates the demand," David Walkden, the chief executive of Glug Ltd, a wine retailer dealing in large quantities of wine, has declared. It's more advantageous to satisfy market demands than propose unknown wines. In this case, it's easy for the sales reps, who just go round collecting orders and deal with familiar labels: all they need to ask their clients is, "What do you need?" In contrast, the early sales reps for Prosecco were introducing wines and producers that were completely unknown. They needed a sense of initiative, the ability to be flexible in making deals, as well as a capacity to talk about health or football. Giuseppe Tomaselli of Enotria claims he knows the medical records of certain clients as well as their GPs do. A good sales rep knows how to reinvent himself so he doesn't become boring and doesn't keep coming out with the same old lines. Riccardo Grigolo from Al Boccon di'vino in Richmond complains that some of them "talk as much as a barber; I hate it if they start telling me about their competitors". Sales reps are trained to keep talking in order to fill up any awkward silences, and sometimes they come out with small talk or bragging. Some fib in order to come over better, but they can be amusing if they do this with irony. Others want to satisfy the expectations of their clients, so say the things they think they want to hear. They don't intend to tell lies: it just happens in the course of talking. But in the end, the successful sale reps are those who know what to leave out, when not to push themselves forward, how to avoid ostentation. Earnest types with bees in their bonnets don't make good sales reps.*

"There are likeable and unlikeable people" is the blunt distinction drawn by Rocco Tanzarella, from the Bottega del Pane in Wimbledon. Usually, good sales reps are good seducers; courtship and selling have some of the same obstacles, as well as the same sense of satisfaction if you're successful. In both situations, Italians use a congenial technique: gallantry. Polite insistence pays off, and good sales reps don't give up: they're like actors who adapt to the role required by the circumstances. At the outset their language changes: it's as if they're reciting a script; as success seems more and more certain, so the language becomes more normal. It can even become vulgar if the client shows no interest and the sales rep isn't much of a gentleman. Sales reps are known for their seduction of women. This is also a "clientele" which has to be continually expanded and changed; a good sales rep never draws the line. "It's a bit like hunting for mushrooms," says Gabriele Nodari. "You never manage to get that last mushroom which would make your satisfaction complete."

Women sales reps

"I believe in transparency and sincerity. These are qualities which really help individuals and companies to grow, but they're only possible if you're capable of appreciating the virtues and accepting the defects of your own collaborators." (Daniela Franchini)

Women who are young and pretty have problems selling wine to Italian restaurants. At the outset they attract attention, and that can have positive results. But restaurateurs are used to flattery, and will immediately show their intentions. The female sales reps will be invited to agree to a kind of bargain. At this point they need to keep their distance, because the restaurateur's insistent approaches can become embarrassing. Giving in to his advances is not a good way to make a career in sales. Women need to know how to defend themselves from the womanizers in the business; older women succeed better if they limit themselves to a friendly openness. Paolo Gasparini, who runs the Giotto restaurant, once told Daniela Franchini, who heads a team of female sales reps: "Don't worry yourself – you're so warm-hearted you'll sell lots of wine even knowing nothing about the business."

"I began work as a sales rep for a wine distributors in 2002," Daniela writes. "At the time, almost all sales reps were men. Restaurateurs were taken aback to see a woman coming in through the door wearing a suit and carrying her cases. You could see in their eyes the difficulty they had in establishing a working relationship with a woman. The only women who worked in restaurants were the waitresses, and some of them were treated badly. Women chefs were not liked because, it was claimed, they didn't work well under pressure. Restaurateurs saw Italian women either as the classic mother and housewife figure or as a kind of toy you could have fun with – or as a psychologist you could tell your frustrations to and get some affection in return. Today the situation is different, and the number of women working as sales reps in the wine business has increased."

"I'm a leader, not a boss. That's why I've never felt alone." (Daniela Franchini)

"I work for Zonin UK, an Italian company with a sales team made up of seven women. Being a female sales rep remains a hard job. I always tell my team to dress and behave in a professional manner. With a female sales rep, a client might place an order immediately, but then he'll invite her to dinner. That's the downside. Women have to earn the client's respect and esteem first, before they clinch a sale, just like male colleagues have to. But there's a positive aspect too: clients are much more ready to listen to a woman. Men are more sensitive when dealing with women; many clients are real gentlemen. Today things have improved; young restaurateurs are much less concerned whether the sales rep is a man or a woman. But men trust a woman more; they feel more secure, as if the situation is more under control. Women tend to be straightforward: they stick to the rules, and clients see they're trustworthy."

Foreign promoters

The Italians who have gone to live outside Italy have communicated to those in their circle their abiding love for their native land, they've formed relationships, they've mixed easily with the races and cultures of their adopted countries. The former boxer Antonio Sorano used to enchant the British with his talk of the sun and sea and food of his native city, Brindisi. One day, in a London bar, the two young women with whom he was in conversation smilingly asked him why he was here: "If Italy's so beautiful, how come you're living in rainy England?" Perhaps Italy doesn't deserve such enthusiastic loyalty, but it's true that Italians living abroad transmit their longing for their homeland, and in the process encourage new foreign-born promoters of

Italian products. The Brazilian Cleide Silva, a professional samba dancer, was inspired to become a seller of Italian wines by a Tuscan friend. Similarly the Chinese Yan Li, who is committed to becoming a Master of Wine. Piers Plowden became fond of Prosecco thanks to a friendship in Asolo in 1997; he went on to set up a small import-and-distribution company with the aim of popularizing the wine that was still quite unfamiliar in the UK market – though later, despite his hard work getting it going, he had to close it down because of disappointing results. The Turkish seller Habibe Direk was in a relationship with a Cypriot who had lived in Italy for several years and had opened various Italian restaurants in London. The Iranian Niloofar Gardner had fallen in love with Italy when she spent time there as a very young girl. Niloofar has become familiar with certain Italian characteristics, including some of their contradictions: "Only a few Italians manage to combine appearance and content, form and substance." She has described her relationship with the country as follows:

"The revolution in Iran in 1979 changed my country for ever, and I found myself living in the UK, where I was studying. Since then I've always suffered from being so far from my native land, and I think back often to my early memories, so sharp and clear, of my formative years. The older I become, the more I search my past, like an archeologist putting fragments together, clues to a way of life and a land which disappeared many years ago and which represent my roots – a place where no one asks you where you come from or how often you go home. It's my grandparents' house I remember most vividly: the hiding places where my grandfather would go to have a quiet smoke; sleeping out in the garden on humid summer nights; the air thick with the perfume of jasmine blossom, which would later be dried for infusions. Outside the familiar walls of home, there were the streets with their cooking aromas, the fragrance of steaming rice and exotic saffron.

"I was constantly looking for pictures that resembled what I had once known, a place where I could redraw the images of those quiet moments again and again. I was looking for a way of unifying that twilit past and the clear present, to see those dreams as realities, even if only for an instant. Italy is the place where this happens; it's like a touchstone, with all its natural beauty, its vitality and its contradictions."

"Every people has its contradictions, but they're more perceptible to foreigners." (Andrea Riva)

Dalbir Singh from India grew interested in Italy after reading a British writer's account of how the geographical differences of Germany and Italy had an effect on their peoples. "I was curious about the differences in mentality – the linear Germans and the complicated and heterogeneous Italians – caused by the contrast between the flat terrain of Germany and the diverse landscape of Italy." Dalbir's curiosity about Italy extended to its cooking, its cinema and opera – and its wine. He specialized in the distribution of wines from small Italian producers, which he selected and marketed in London from 1990 onwards.* "One day Italian wines will be the best in the world. History, so far, has proved me right." And he adds: "Italy has a great food culture, and Italians are in part aware of its potential, but at times they're blinded by the love of their own cuisine and don't appreciate what's good in the food of other countries." Dalbir finds Prosecco an interesting product, in that its growing success foreshadows some of the insidious challenges of the future: "If you increase quantity without paying attention to quality, you'll sell well in the short term, but in the long run you'll fail."

Roger Nyeko's journey to the unknown

"I was born in Uganda, where the best of Africa is concentrated. It's a land with extraordinary mountains, the 'Mountains of the Moon', as well as other natural marvels alongside a happy and friendly people. My journey into the unknown started because I wanted to find out about new realities, and it materialized thanks to a happy coincidence, a sort of lucky blessing. The country was sliding into political instability when I was selected to go on a study course in Italy. It was a time when the Italian Government had launched a campaign to win the hearts of people in our regions, which were still subject to British rule. My journey began with a flight over the Nile towards the Mediterranean."

"The Nile runs through a spectacular landscape that looks like an oil painting, across winding marshes, plains, savannahs and rolling hills; a land where the highest concentration of primates in the world is found, including the majestic gorilla." (Roger Nyeko)

"We landed in Rome. By good fortune, while I was attending the school, I was able to visit the houses of my new Italian classmates. The boys and girls invited me back to their homes for meals. I learnt to make gnocchi and grew to like my coffee with the *resentin*, when the coffee cup is rinsed with a drop of grappa after drinking the coffee. I learnt the language and the customs, and I enjoyed the long hours spent at the table over meals. For many of my new friends it was the first time they'd ever mixed with a black man. The girls liked me and found me well-mannered. The life and culture of this part of Italy changed my world, and I came to love the people and their way of life. From one region to the next there was always something different and interesting. Of course, while we were living there, some of my fellow Ugandans had some bad moments, when they were discriminated against and insulted. I was lucky though – the families of my friends always had good words to say about me. One of my schoolteachers, who also became a kind of mentor to me, once saw me getting close to an Italian girl and told me the saying *"moglie e buoi dei paesi tuoi"* ("choose wife and cattle from your own village"). A little

later he told me: "Nyeko, you didn't listen to me." But he
came to my wedding to Silvana, a curly-haired, blue-eyed
blonde from Adria in the Veneto.

"Afterwards I moved to England, where I immediately had
the idea of turning my passion for Italy into a wine-related
business.* So I took on this new challenge, which seemed
natural and doable because I had so many vivid memories.
Now when I go back to visit my family in Uganda they call
me the "Italian" – and the British too call me 'Roger the
Italian'. In the Veneto, where we have a house, whenever
I go back my friends greet me with a 'Ciao, bello', which
always touches me and reflects my way of being. My work
is very close to my heart: I am entirely focused on selling
Italian products."

Giuseppe Bagatti

Antonio Melina

Alvaro Maccioni

Giuliano Ferrari

The picturesque "rive" of Valdobbiadene

Attilio, Emilio, Sergio e Giovanni Mionetto

Carlo Cataldi e
Gian Piero Gorietti

Lorenzo e Mara Berni

Enzo Di Nolfi e Franco Merloni

Alessandro, Carlo e Marcello Di Stefano

Angelo Camassa

Domenico Taravella

Teo Catino

Enzo Cassini

Gianni Segatta

Lord Charles Forte

Daniela Franchini

Roger Nyeko

Lucio Altana

Paolo Mancassola

Luigi Colazzo

Pasquale Sarpi

Roberto Gardetto

Roberto Simeone

Luisa Dalla Costa

Pietro De Cesare

Riccardo Grigolo

Sergio De Luca

PART THREE

Early clients

Antonio Carluccio, who ran the Neal Street restaurant in Covent Garden, ordered a large consignment of Prosecco at the end of the 1980s. During a meeting, he politely expressed his pessimism about the wine's chances of success: "Prosecco won't really go down well in Britain." But Augusto Giussani, known as Gas, a former sales rep for Enotria and a trailblazer full of optimism, perceptively predicted that Prosecco "had what it takes to please the English; it's got a great future". Aldo Zilli, from the Abruzzo, then a handsome young man making a career for himself, included Prosecco on the wine list of his restaurant Signor Zilli in Dean Street, London. The restaurant closed down in 1990, but Aldo promised that the restaurants he was planning to open would still include Prosecco. The new Zilli Bar employed a young, professionally trained barman from Asolo, Simon Piovesan, who was attached to his native region and a keen promoter of its products. The restaurant Vecchia Riccione in Covent Garden tried out an innovative way of operating: until midnight it functioned like a normal restaurant, then the lights were lowered, music was played and the clients, together with the staff, rushed onto the dancefloor. According to Giancarlo Fabbris, one of the proprietors grew rich and decided to change the formula: "I'm going to turn the Vecchia Riccione into a serious restaurant." He redecorated the space with a view to attracting a prestigious clientele. But the new restaurant folded after a few months, the owner was left in debt and Prosecco lost one of its best clients. The Tuscan Alvaro Maccioni managed La Famiglia in Chelsea and was keen on introducing new things, including Prosecco. He was looked on as a kind of ambassador for Italian cuisine, and he'd spent many years promoting Italian food and wines. In the 1960s he was the manager of La Terrazza in Soho, and went on to own various restaurants over the following decades.* He was stubborn when it came to getting what he wanted, but his ready smile won hearts. It was Alvaro who was supposed to have said famously: "I tell my chefs that if they cook like their mothers they're good cooks; if they cook like their grandmothers they're great ones." It's a striking remark, and a true one, since hunger makes food taste better, and the shortage of food between the two world wars made even uncooked potatoes taste delicious. Prosecco had a stroke of luck with Alberto Pagano, owner of Il Cappuccetto,* which opened in London in 1962. Alberto saw the brochure publicizing the bottle and said: "That's what I've been looking for." Alberto was from Liguria and loved sailing; he spent a holiday in Italy with friends, during which he drank only Prosecco. He was the founder and for a long time the charismatic president of the Italian Golf Society, and he always urged members to try out Prosecco.

Lino Quaradeghini has been a restaurateur since the 1950s; he started up La Spezia near London Bridge and the Taberna Etrusca in the neighbourhood of St Paul's Cathedral. In the 1980s he handed over the running of the two restaurants to his sons Piero and Enzo. Piero and Enzo responded favourably when Prosecco was pitched to them, and ordered large quantities, at the same time asking their staff to promote the new sparkling wine to the diners.*

Pizza Pucci* on the King's Road included Prosecco on its list as the house sparkling wine. The two owners, Giuseppe Albanese (known as Pucci) and Lilli Malcarne, came from Brindisi in Puglia; Carlo Cataldi once remarked that you could write a book about their lives. The staff of Pizza Pucci, supervised by Sebastiano D'Agostaro, always proposed Prosecco whenever customers asked for a sparkling wine – including champagne. Lilli used to say that "for yuppies, Prosecco is the kind of champagne they like". A seller once spent half a day trying to sell a dozen bottles to Martano Marismari, the owner of the San Rocco restaurant in Sheen. Marismari took the bottles, but didn't succeed in selling a single one for over a year, until one day a customer, originally from Treviso, started to come in and wanted to drink Prosecco with every meal. The same client also went to Pitagora in Richmond, owned by Gino De Siena, and Mario Pagetti's Signor Sassi in Knightsbridge.

Clients from the Veneto

Italians from the Veneto had no reason to go and work abroad in the 1980s. Their own region offered them work and leisure, good food, lots of sunshine, the sea and the mountains near at hand – all this they could enjoy as much as they wanted. But there are many Italians from the Veneto in the UK, and the main reason they've left such a beautiful and prosperous place to come to a rainy island is to learn English. There are other reasons too, of course. From the point of view of industry, the Veneto is a very active region, but it suffers from the limitations that affect Italian industry as a whole. The entrepreneurial opportunities open to youngsters in Italy are often tied to what their fathers do – they follow in their footsteps, and that doesn't always encourage innovation. In Britain individuals have the freedom to change – and they know it. Failure is not a disaster, but rather a possibility of trying again, and people do keep trying again, avoiding past mistakes. Yet, for Italians who live abroad, their sense of pride draws them together; when they come from the same region, such as the Veneto, there's a very strong sense of belonging. All the Italians from the Veneto who were living in the UK were willing to help promote Prosecco.* The restaurateur Enzo Cecconi could have done a bit more; it's true he wasn't from the Veneto, but he had worked in the Hotel Cipriani in Venice. His Mayfair restaurant, Cecconi's, somewhat resembled Harry's Bar in Venice; it was one of the most celebrated Italian restaurants in the 1980s. "My customers only drink champagne," Cecconi told Enzo Mion, from Venice, who even then was a strong believer in the Prosecco of Valdobbiadene, and was trying hard to promote it. Cecconi's bought grappa, but delayed making a decision to include Prosecco on the wine list for some years. Mr Cecconi's air of superiority was justified in the restaurant business, but not when it came to sport, according to some of his colleagues: "Great restaurateur, mediocre golfer." Le Gavroche, a famous French restaurant in London, acquired Prosecco thanks to the manager Silvano Giraldin, from Padua, who used it in Bellini cocktails. The Trevisan Enzo Bucciol, of the Bistro Balzac in Shepherd's Bush, bought supplies of Prosecco regularly; his cellar housed his collection of important French wines, whereas he drank Prosecco as his personal aperitif or used it to make kir royale. Another Paduan, Gianfranco Carraro, was the first restaurateur to serve Prosecco by the glass in his restaurant in Battersea, Carraro's, where he also tried to devise an innovative menu. Mario Arricale worked for a couple of years in Carraro's and considers Gianfranco to be a real pioneer of new Italian culinary ideas: "We thought him a great restaurateur; he may not have achieved the results he wanted, but he made an important contribution to the way things are today." In more recent years, Carraro became a seller for the wine distributor Fiandaca. Claudio Pulze and Franco Zanellato, from the province of Padua, included Prosecco on the wine list of their Chelsea restaurant, The Waterfront. Pulze was keen to expand, and over the course of three decades acquired numerous restaurants.* Iginio Santin, from Jesolo, the owner of Santini on Ebury Street and L'Incontro on Pimlico Road, both in London, immediately agreed to include Prosecco on the wine lists; nowadays he goes around boasting, in dialect: "*Go fatto tutto mi.*" ("I did it all myself!") Toni Piron, from Padua, of Toni's Brasserie in Hammersmith, ordered Prosecco principally for himself. He was proud of having worked as a maître d' in Arab countries, and had come to share their outlook: "You can get anything if you're prepared to pay for it." Gianni Pauro, of the restaurant Formula Veneta, didn't particularly like Prosecco, but he loved the idea that it came from the Veneto. Gianni is full of vitality, a real live wire. The wine-seller Remo Casadei once compared him to lightning; his presence always creates a bit of a buzz. Gianni is really knowledgeable about wine. Unlike many wine experts, who are only introduced to wine when they are adults, Gianni began to drink as a child in his family's café in Padua: "It's like sport: when you learn as a child, you're always a step ahead."

Some restaurateurs

Lorenzo and Mara Berni,
Osteria San Lorenzo

"I met Mara Berni for the first time many years ago, when she said to me: "That's a nice jacket you're wearing – it suits you" – and then she massaged my shoulder a little. That's an encounter I've never forgotten." (Enzo Cassini)

"The global launch of Prosecco took place in the Osteria San Lorenzo" – so Lorenzo Berni declares.* And if it's true what Stefano Cadamuro has said – "All fashions start in London" – then the Osteria San Lorenzo has certainly played a part. Over the course of the decades it's been in business, it has attracted a high-profile international clientele. From the very day Prosecco started to be sold in the UK market, San Lorenzo has displayed a bottle on its bar. The Osteria opened in 1963 in Beauchamp Place, in the heart of Knightsbridge; just a few tables, like a small family trattoria, presided over by the owners Lorenzo Berni and his wife Mara. Diners Club didn't allow them to use their credit-card system, as they thought the restaurant's turnover would be too small. From that day on, Lorenzo refused to take credit cards, out of principle: they shouldn't have turned a business down for being too small and therefore all the more in need of support. Right from the outset, the menu offered a range of popular Italian dishes: *bollito misto*, stewed rabbit with polenta, *coda alla vaccinara*, *trippa alla mentuccia*, *cotechino con lenticchie e bagna cauda*. The restaurant got off to a good start and expanded, though it kept the typical dishes on the menu. It was frequented by famous clients – politicians, footballers and musicians from all over the world. Ordinary customers rubbed shoulders with famous personalities, young and old, from music, cinema and sport. There are not many restaurants which have such a glorious and prestigious history as the Osteria San Lorenzo. It is a unique fairy tale. The Sardinian manager Domenico Loi remarked that it was "a combination of circumstances generated by various factors working together which can never be repeated". Lorenzo has worked in France, but he contrasted Italian cooking "*della mamma*" with French cuisine "of the chefs". A Frenchman once told him that "Italian cooking was women's cooking", to which Lorenzo replied: "*Pas de* femmes, *mais c'est la cuisine de* mammes." His great achievement stems from his conviction that Italian cooking is healthy: "Your mum loves you; she'd never betray you or do you harm. A mother nourishes her children with food that tradition and experience have shown to be beneficial." Armed with this truth, Lorenzo has followed his own path, ignoring the opinion of the media and of fashionable restaurants. The dishes served in the Osteria San Lorenzo are based on his childhood memories of what he ate when growing up at Forte dei Marmi in Versilia. There was the sea, and there was maize, and there were peas. At low tide the inhabitants would gather small cuttlefish and squid, which they would cook with polenta. Berni was unique in offering a traditional cuisine to clients used to eating more elaborate and sophisticated dishes. The way the food is presented is informal, and Lorenzo's relaxed face puts everyone at ease. Fifty years of success haven't changed him; he still moves among the tables telling anecdotes to a well-disposed clientele, as if the restaurant were a stage. The reality of celebrities and of politicians is artificial; San Lorenzo is an opportunity to test the personalities of these figures who are playing their part in the human comedy. But Lorenzo and Mara* have a code of conduct which you rarely see, and which does them great honour. When Princess Diana – who was a regular customer – died, they refused to allow journalists from the Italian state television to come and film, out of respect for her. "You don't publicize the misfortunes of others." The journalists filmed the Osteria from the outside, and reported that it was so exclusive they had been denied access.

For Lorenzo the new sparkling wine suited his restaurant very well. He made the decision to take it and offer it to his clients. If Lorenzo supported the cause, then it was obvious that success would come sooner or later – he had a magic touch. In 2011 a famous personage who lived in Monte Carlo came to eat at the Osteria. Lorenzo asked him if he would like a glass of champagne, to which the customer replied, unexpectedly: "I'd prefer a glass of Prosecco." Lorenzo instinctively punched the air, just as he'd done when Italy won the World Cup final against France in 2006. "We've done it!" he exclaimed.

Giuseppe Battocchi and La Taverna

Originally from Como, Giuseppe Battocchi – known as Peppino – worked for a while at the Goring Hotel in Belgravia, before opening the La Taverna restaurant in Windsor in 1962, not far from the Castle.* In 1969 he opened a second restaurant, Don Peppino, nearby. In 1989 he was getting tired of working and had lost interest in innovation: he felt he had done his bit for his home country, and it was time to take a rest. But Peppino, who has a rather aristocratic habit of pronouncing his Rs the French way, is, despite himself, very attached to his profession, and passionate too about Italian food and drink. He already knew about Carpenè Malvolti, and asked to know more about Prosecco. In the end he couldn't stop himself from taking on new commitments to promote the wine in his restaurant. Being led by some involuntary force has been the story of his life: he came to England at the end of the 1950s to stay six months and learn the language. For reasons he can't explain, he ended up staying on, and had the most varied experiences – but he's always felt as if he's in Britain just temporarily. Now he feels as if the restaurant has him captive. He's not at ease, and keeps worrying about the customers, and serving them with great attentiveness. It's a kind of illness, as he's well aware, and one for which it's difficult to find a cure. He himself says with a melancholy air: "Look at me – I'm still doing what I was doing sixty years ago – and what I was going to give up doing after six months!"

Giuliano Ferrari of Villa Bianca

Giuliano Ferrari, born in Cremona, remarks that "all the Italians involved in the restaurant business who came to Britain in the 1960s were trained in large hotels". He himself, after experiences in several large hotels across Europe, came to England in 1963, where he worked for three years at the Savoy Hotel. In 1967 he opened Il Rugantino; the name evoked the restaurant with the same name in Rome, which was notorious for a scandal involving some celebrities. In 1969, in partnership with the Cypriot businessman Angelo Costa, Giuliano founded the Villa Bianca in Hampstead, which quickly became very successful. He took on Prosecco and Cartizze enthusiastically; like a true professional, he believed in "selling what he liked to his customers". His friend Carlo Petitto says that "for Giuliano, what's important are his friends, good food, good wine and women. At the end of the evening, when all the diners had gone home, he would stay on in the restaurant until morning playing cards with other restaurateurs." He's also keen on horse-racing and gambling. He once bought a racehorse and named it Villa Bianca; the only time the horse ever won a race, Giuliano forgot to place a bet on it. Gambling is an expensive pastime, but he smiles and denies having any regrets. Carlo Petitto remarks: "All emigrants deep inside are gamblers; all the Italians of Giuliano's generation were." To his peers, fearful of losing the wealth they've acquired, Giuliano's grin seems to say "It's easier to relax when you don't have so much" – so long as you have friends, you're in good health, and you can lead a dignified life independent of how much money you've got – or haven't. Today Giuliano is still working as a consultant and managing director of restaurants.

Gianni Rossi of Bucci

Gianni left his home town of Bardi in 1965 and came to London because he wanted to see a girl again, Sandra, his future wife, who'd gone there. He relates what happened: "I didn't have the slightest intention of staying in England. I was getting on just fine in Italy. But a mishap altered my plans. Sandra became pregnant. What could I do? Ask my dad for help? No way, it was my problem. My sense of pride means I either go down or I make a success of it by myself. I once took Sandra to Harrods. We couldn't afford a thing. I told her: 'One day I'll bring you back here and you'll be able to buy what you want.' So we went to Fortnum & Mason instead and bought a small box of *marrons glacés*, which we had eaten by the time we got home. Then our son Stefano was born – I needed to start working and earning. My first job was laying rubber flooring for Pirelli. That was too hard. So I went to an employment agency for Italians and told them I was looking for work as a dishwasher in Italian restaurants. 'No,' Felice in their office told me. 'You're a good-looking guy, and you should be working front of house." But it was hard to find a stable job, because the owners didn't like the fact I had no experience as a waiter. Then I bumped into Piero Rossi, known as 'Barolo', from Como, who thought only of Barolo, polenta and pheasants. He liked the fact we shared the same surname, so he gave me the opportunity to learn. With a bank loan I bought a house which needed a lot of work doing on it. I was quoted £7,000, which I thought crazy, so in my spare time I started to do the work myself. It went really well, and from then on friends and acquaintances in the business would give me building jobs they needed doing in their homes or restaurants. In about 1975 I built my first restaurant, Sambuca, commissioned by Sandro Tobi and Mario Pagetti. Then I built and launched and eventually sold on my own restaurants; they were all called Bucci, which was how we nicknamed my second son Gianni junior.* I remember the opening night of the first Bucci. I was inexperienced and hadn't made the right preparations. There were too many customers, and I didn't have time to calculate and write all the bills. So I just asked everyone there to tot up themselves what they thought they owed me. It wasn't a bad idea, as it turned out – the restaurant got a reputation as a place where you only paid what you thought was the fair price." Today Gianni keeps as busy and as youthful as ever, enjoying himself as a construction entrepreneur.

Gino Taddei of Cibo

When he was young, Gino Taddei worked in a bank in Genoa. The chief cashier told him he'd have to wait thirty years before he'd get promotion, but Gino couldn't wait that long, so left his secure job in Italy for an uncertain future elsewhere. He first worked as a dishwasher at the Hard Rock Café in London. After six months, he was promoted to making the sandwiches, and then he was made grill chef. After two years, he moved to the restaurant Eleven Park Walk in London. The owner, Franco Zanellato, from Padua, taught him the profession. Then in 1986 Gino and his wife Sally travelled to Toronto, New York and Sydney, where they did various jobs, finally returning to London, where in 1989 in partnership with the chef Claudio Pegoraro, from the Veneto, he opened Cibo between Olympia and Holland Park. At first, business was slow; the bored staff spent their time fine-tuning the décor. Then a favourable review in the *Evening Standard* changed everything. The restaurant had a number of original features at the time: a limited menu of regional dishes served on large, brightly coloured terracotta plates. The following year Gino set up L'Altro, a fish restaurant in Portobello, before any of the other restaurants that would populate the area were started. A welcoming glass of Prosecco has always been offered to diners. Gino knows a lot about Italian cuisine, and regularly eats in other restaurants. He dislikes being confused with those promoters of Italian food who are only in the business for the profits they can make.*

Andrea Riva of Riva

Andrea Riva opened Riva restaurant in 1990 in Barnes in the suburbs of London. It was a small place with an original and restrained décor. It immediately got good reviews in the press; *Time Out* voted it Best Italian Restaurant of the Year. It soon attracted the kind of prestigious clientele that successful restaurants aspire to. Among its customers were also some influential people in the wine business, such as the consultant Bill Baker, who promoted Prosecco in the UK restaurant trade. Andrea presented Prosecco to the Conran Group, to his friend Eddie Lim from Singapore who managed the Deals restaurant chain in partnership with Lord Lichfield and Viscount Linley, to Antony Worrall Thompson's One Ninety One, to the distributors Machiavelli, who specialized in "niche" food products, and to other restaurateurs with international staff and cuisine from a range of countries, who liked this new sparkling wine. Riva restaurant became a model for a new generation of restaurateurs emerging in those years.

Andrea carefully chooses the people he wants to talk to. He's a cultivated man and likes to converse with his customers on the most disparate topics, from football to music, history to philosophy. He sees his restaurant a bit like the bistros of the Boulevard Saint-Germain in Paris, where early-twentieth-century French intellectuals would congregate. By the table in the corner where he usually sits there are two shelves of books, which he sometimes quotes from to back up his arguments. He comes out with acute aphorisms and witty remarks; he has the unusual ability to shape the world around him. He resisted any temptation to open a larger restaurant in a more central area of London, believing being small doesn't prevent you from being great. He's created the right-sized restaurant in which he can converse with the kind of clientele he wants.

"Home cooking is best: you don't really eat well elsewhere. I've spent a lot of time teaching my wife how to cook, and now I really only want to eat at home." (Giorgio Giusto)

Ossie Gray of the River Café

In 1987 two distinguished ladies, with contacts in Tuscany, opened the River Café, an Italian restaurant with no Italian staff. Rose Gray and Ruth Rogers were inspired by Italian home cooking; they would visit friends in

Tuscany and meticulously collect recipes. Their idea was to use the best ingredients available and the traditional techniques of Italian cooking. People usually go out to eat in restaurants precisely because they couldn't have that kind of cooking at home, but the River Café takes the opposite view: it offers you authentic Italian family cooking, with no frills or artifice. For thirty years it's been popular with a numerous clientele and has received warm reviews in the press. The restaurant, managed by the two women who came into the business in middle age, even though expensive, is known for the honesty of its cooking, quite different from the kind of artificial cooking concocted by pretentious chefs. There are no dressed-up waiters trying to persuade and win clients over; the food itself takes centre stage. Ossie Gray, Rose's son, looked after the wine list.* He knew about Prosecco and understood what kind of wine it is and why it's popular. The best Prosecco for him is the "*frizzante*", lightly sparkling kind: "Unlike champagne, Prosecco is good to drink at all times of day." So it was highlighted on the wine list and sold at a reasonable price. In the River Café it's the wine which is drunk most and on all occasions; Ruth's husband, the architect Lord Richard Rogers, has also been involved in giving the wine exposure at social events – a free and invaluable publicity for Prosecco.

Arnoldo and Franco of Florians

Two business partners, Arnoldo Onisto, known as Arnie, from Asolo in the Veneto, and Franco Papa, a Sicilian from Palazzolo Acreide, were the owners of Florians in Crouch End, in North London. It opened in 1989. The restaurant was divided into two spaces: the dining room and an area for the bar. The two men got on well, and their characters complemented each other: Arnie was a hard worker, always on the move, while Franco liked to joke and laugh. The restaurant and bar became a kind of club for a large number of regular clients in the neighbourhood. It felt a bit like *EastEnders*, with its daily cast of characters. Clients would meet at Florians, like members of one big family, to tell their troubles and find someone to listen to them; there was always someone to help – not in the sense that they solved really serious problems, but to offer human solidarity. In the interval between lunch and dinner, the chefs would try out new dishes, which the regulars would sample. After encountering some initial reluctance, Prosecco won their favour. Arnie was able to communicate his passion for food and wine to those around him; Franco was entertained by how he managed to do it. The pair of them acted like a magnet for people from Crouch End and the surrounding area.*

138

Because of its success at Florians, nearby restaurants also started to order in Prosecco. One of these was the Bouzy Rouge, owned by Roger Robar, from Martinique, who ordered large supplies of the wine. When the restaurant first opened, Roger was the chef – he had three children to maintain and needed to work hard. One fine day in 1996 he won £5.8 million playing the National Lottery; he became known for this stroke of extraordinary good luck. He bought the restaurant where he worked, gave money to his children and was extremely generous to friends and former colleagues. He told the *Independent* newspaper that he'd given away over one and a half million to people who had written to him asking for help, adding: "I paid off the debts and mortgages of my colleagues, and I helped a woman who claimed she had an incurable illness. As soon as they had the money, I didn't see them again. I'm someone who thinks you should give what you receive, but even just a phone call to thank me would have been nice." Roger thought that he had been chosen by destiny, and that he should show the qualities of a good businessman. His good nature, however, was at odds with his ambitions. He sold the restaurant and now thinks he's bound to win the lottery a second time.

Franco and Ann Taruschio of The Walnut Tree

"I am a *conte* ('count') of little consequence," Franco Taruschio, who's carried the gospel of Italian food into

Wales, used to joke.* He takes *conte* to be short for *contadino* or "farmer", since that was his background in the Marche region. Having worked in various European cities, in 1961 he came to Britain, where he met his future wife Ann. They married at the young age of twenty-four. In 1963 they bought a small pub, The Walnut Tree, in the Welsh countryside, near Abergavenny. In the early years they served French cuisine, since, according to Franco, "the war was still a recent memory, and they didn't think much of Italians round here". Later on they switched to Italian food, with dishes that made use of the fresh ingredients that were available. Franco remembers how as a boy his mother would watch him while he ate: "I had to finish everything on the plate, since it was good, and it did me good, and you didn't throw anything away." By observing his fellow townspeople as a boy, Franco learnt how to use local ingredients, such as herbs or anything else that was edible, in their cooking. Ann and Franco deserve credit not only for introducing Italian cooking to Wales, but for using the same approach to ingredients they found in Wales which many of the locals didn't know they could use.

Paolo Nolasco remembers that "like the Osteria San Lorenzo, The Walnut Tree didn't accept credit cards. But unlike the Osteria, there were no cash machines in the vicinity, just hills and trees and sheep. But the experience of eating there was worth the drive..." Ann and Franco have done a lot of research on food and cooking, publishing six books, taking part in television programmes and teaching in schools. Franco was given an OBE in 2003 for services to the restaurant business. Now he and his wife are both retired,* but their house in Abergavenny is always open to their friends, and also to strangers, a place of conversation and sociability, a delight for the senses and the spirit.

Giuseppe and Pamela Turi of Enoteca Turi

Giuseppe Turi didn't achieve his ambitions in Puglia, where he was born; instead, together with his wife Pamela, it was in London that he fulfilled his dreams. "I was twenty-nine and, professionally, didn't have many opportunities, so I decided to go into the high-end restaurant business. I started as a waiter at the Athenaeum Hotel, and after three years became a sommelier and was taken on at the Connaught Hotel. Then I returned to the Athenaeum as restaurant manager until 1990. In those eight years I learnt a lot about flavours and aromas, as well as getting to know some extraordinary products. It really was an unknown world, with its history and culture and traditions, and one where real improvements could also be made. I discovered French wines, so popular with the European aristocracy, and French cuisine, of which the traditions were often influenced by the culinary habits of the old Italian noble families.

"In 1990 I realized there was room for improvement in the cuisine on offer in Italian restaurants in London. The wine lists were very limited too. So I opened Enoteca Turi in Putney, with the aim that the cooking and the

wines we offered would reflect the new developments
then taking place. But it also dawned on me how little I
knew about Italy and its cuisine. So I started a journey
of research and discovery. I grew to see Italy as a nation
embracing a variety of regions, forming a mosaic of
differences and similarities – a nation where the cooking contained, so to speak, the genetic imprint of each
regional history. The world of Italian wine has undergone an evolution, thanks to people who have acted as
a guide to an entire generation. It's been a privilege for
me to belong to this community. This has enabled me
to get to know so many Italians who transmit a sense
of our country's extraordinarily rich heritage of food
and wine."

Teo Catino of Pagliaccio

Teo Catino was born in Irpinia in southern Italy. He used
to sell T-shirts and socks on a London street stall, then in
1992 he got involved in managing Il Pagliaccio in Fulham.
The choice of the name, which means "clown" in Italian,
was appropriate. The intention was to create an enjoyable
ambience, where the staff weren't too serious and where, if
anyone complained, you could always respond by pointing
to the restaurant's name. The Pagliaccio is lively and noisy;
the sound of Teo's voice booming out makes you think of
the street markets you find in Italian squares. Teo has done
a lot to make his restaurant part of the local community

in Fulham. He used to drink Prosecco at Casa Carlo, and when his own restaurant opened, he made it a wine for all occasions. He didn't have any experience as a restaurateur, so he took some risky decisions at first. In the 1990s he ordered four pallets of Prosecco – 2,400 bottles – in order to get a discount on the total sale price. When the order was delivered, he realized there wasn't enough room in the cellar, so put the boxes under the tables, in the office, on the stairs, next to the toilets. Customers were automatically offered a glass of Prosecco when they came in, presumably in an attempt to get rid of the boxes they would otherwise have tripped over. But Teo managed to shift the order in a very brief space of time, thanks to Il Pagliaccio's marketing techniques. Passers-by are courteously assailed and proffered a coffee or a glass of Prosecco. Two young waiters, elegantly dressed and holding a bottle and an ice bucket, would offer glasses to passengers waiting at a nearby bus stop. Teo also owns two other restaurants. He was once interviewed on the BBC, and when the interviewer asked him why he ran more than one restaurant he replied: "I've got two children and a beautiful wife of whom I'm proud – but they are very expensive." Teo has allowed Il Pagliaccio to be used for gala evenings in support of the Marsden Hospital, which specializes in cancer treatment, and has collected large sums of money for the cause.

"Fish should evoke the taste of the sea – if it doesn't, choose the meat instead." (Angelo Colao)

Gina and Franco Santoro of Casa Mamma

If you eat good fish, then the Prosecco you drink with it will taste even better. Casa Mamma in King's Cross opened in 1994; the menu offers flavourful fish which conjures up the aroma of sea salt. You almost think the sea is just outside the front door, instead of cars stuck in traffic round King's Cross Station. Franco and Gina are from Salerno, and on the menu you can find fresh sardines, shipped in directly from the Amalfi Coast, together with baby squid and peas, grilled prawns, *vongole veraci* and mussels cooked with tomatoes. Franco Santoro, a man of few words, knows what good cooking is about. The menu evokes the Mediterranean. You don't get the seabass or gilthead that look dull, as though they've been embalmed, which you find elsewhere in London, served in small portions on a bed of potatoes or with a few leaves of rocket scattered on top. The taste of fish should evoke the sea and never be mixed up with vegetables and other ingredients. As Gina says, "You should do as little as possible to fish!" Gina's mother, Raffaella Novi, came to England in 1951, and was one of the first people to introduce Italian cooking into the country. She managed the Montegrappa restaurant in Fulham from 1967 onwards.

Gianfranco Cioffi of Zero

Gianfranco's mother's family had been in the restaurant business since 1870. Gianfranco went to catering college and, after graduating, together with a friend, looked for work in hotels in northern Italy. He had problems getting a job, because he didn't speak English. So, in 1973, he hitch-hiked his way to England. In London he worked as a chef in Gennaro's in Soho. A year later he moved to Dolce Notte in Jermyn Street. He opened his first restaurant in 1983 in Wood Green. Then he moved to Cockfosters, where he called the new restaurant The Italian Touch. In 1991 the salesman Giuseppe Tomaselli introduced him to Prosecco; Gianfranco noticed that his customers preferred it to Lambrusco. "The bubbles make it easy to drink; some people like it more than champagne. Unlike other sparkling wines, you can drink two or three glasses of Prosecco at a sitting." In 2005 he sold the restaurant for a good sum of money; his idea was to live off the proceeds. At the same time, his sister, who was a business consultant in Ravello, persuaded him to come back to Italy and invest his money in a luxury hotel. "Don't worry," she told him, "it's a winner." Gianfranco was attracted by the idea of a large-scale new project and invested all his money. Before the hotel even opened, the tax authorities opened an investigation, because a magistrate suspected irregularities in the provenance of the money. Gianfranco had to start lengthy legal proceedings before the hotel could open; he eventually won the case after a very hard battle, but, demoralized and frustrated, he decided to pack it all in and return to England. He opened a new restaurant in Hertfordshire and called it Zero, because that was what he felt like. But the restaurant was successful, and nowadays he's certain of one thing: "I'm never going back to Italy, not even in a coffin."

Domenico Taravella of Il Tamburino

Domenico was born in Palermo and has been living in England since 1998. He went to a hospitality and catering college back in Sicily, but decided to leave the island, which he loves but also defines as "scorched earth", to find work in northern Italy, from the holiday spots of Piedmont across to the Dolomites. But he had no luck, for the usual reason that he didn't speak English. So he left Italy and flew to London on his own. His flight landed at Stansted, and after a week he found a job as a dishwasher in an Italian restaurant, Il Tarantino, near the airport. After a few months, he was promoted to waiter. Later he applied to become the manager of a restaurant in Somerset, also belonging to the owner of Tarantino. No one knew anything about Italian cooking or about Prosecco in the villages of Somerset. Domenico introduced *calzoni*, *cannoli* and other Sicilian dishes. The wine list included – in addition to Insolia and Nero d'Avola

– Prosecco, which is as popular in Sicily as it is in the Veneto. Today Domenico runs four Tamburino restaurants, three of which he owns outright, while the fourth is in partnership. He employs young Italians, and is gradually introducing more and more of the locals to Italian food. "I put my heart and soul into what I do. I'm not like the businessmen who run restaurant chains and are just interested in making money." But he also knows that his restaurants will eventually interest the big chains as they seek to expand. For the moment, in the twenty-first century, Domenico personifies the spirit of the early Italian migrants. He's ready to take on new challenges without too much calculation. "It's like when we went diving in Sicily. You knew there were rocks below the water, but if you think about them you'll never dive. We never gave them a thought."*

Arrigo Cipriani of C. London

"Now I come to think about it, writing this, it seems odd to me that I've found out about the world not because I've gone and seen it, but because the world came to find me…" (Arrigo Cipriani)*

The restaurant C. London is managed by the Cipriani family. It was initially called Cipriani, but after a long legal battle on the commercial rights to the name, Arrigo Cipriani was forced to take down the sign with his famous surname. C. London has an international clientele, and its menu reflects the long family tradition. It opened in 2005 in Mayfair, a stone's throw from Berkeley Square. It's a replica of Harry's Bar in Venice and of all the other restaurants all over the world – especially in the US – managed by Arrigo and his son Giuseppe. Arrigo is the son of Giuseppe Cipriani, who is reputed to have created the Bellini cocktail* and carpaccio.* In his restaurants customers can discover a new meaning of the word "restore": to offer relief. Ermanno Taverna is moved whenever he eats here; he finds the excellent service, the soothing atmosphere, the skill in making customers feel at their ease that were common in bygone times. It reminds him of old times at the Savoy Hotel, and when he goes he always leaves a generous tip. The managers of the Cipriani restaurant – Carlo Proietti, Marco Boito, Riccardo Quacquarelli and Federico Bonetti* – confirm that Arrigo's restaurant is the best school of hospitality there is: "Arrigo is the top." The vintner Gennaro Politelli explains: "The Cipriani family has made Harry's Bar as famous as the Rialto Bridge or St Mark's Basilica all over the world, but, as Arrigo says, in the end it's just a room." C. London is where the largest quantity of Prosecco is drunk, mostly in Bellinis.

Lucio Altana of Lucio

When, in 1972, Lucio Altana left his home town, the Sardinian port city of Olbia, his father Mario told him: "Don't become disillusioned, and don't disappoint me:

work hard and be honest." After many years working at the Osteria San Lorenzo, Lucio decided to take on a new challenge. In 2003 he opened Lucio on Fulham Road in Chelsea. It's a very good area, but recent history wasn't promising: several restaurateurs had tried to open in the very same building, but had failed to make their businesses a success. A few days after the opening, the restaurant critic A.A. Gill wrote a review in *The Sunday Times*, pouring contempt on the service and predicting that the place would only last a few months, without a glimmer of understanding or patience for this newcomer on the scene. But Lucio was determined and convinced he could make it, and the restaurant gradually became better known – and then more and more crowded. As it was near to Chelsea stadium, footballers and other people associated with the sport went to eat there. Lucio's success is down to his idea of what a restaurant is about: "The customer is king, and everything must be done to make him feel at ease." In a short space of time, the restaurant started to attract a prestigious clientele, who found it offered a reliable and discreet service and ambience. A lot of business lunches and dinners take place there, and clients trust in Lucio's sense of reserve. He even mediates between businessmen who wish to get to know each other; a word to him either directly or on the phone is enough to sound out the possibility of a meeting. But Lucio's professionalism shows itself in the way he knows when to draw the line and not intrude further on his clients' private affairs, and they respect him for it and treat him as an equal. The restaurant is run by Lucio and his family: his wife Jaca and sons Dario and Mirco. The British like family-run Italian restaurants and reward Lucio for his hard work.

Pizza Express

Pizza has something in common with Prosecco: people like it immediately, but unlike the wine, the Italians themselves only benefit partially in economic terms. Foreigners are the main players. The first pizzeria in London, as Lorenzo Berni recalls, was La Romanella Pizza Express on Wardour Street in Soho. It opened in 1960 under the ownership of the film director Mario Zampi, who'd asked a well-known chef in Rome called Rastelli to come over and work for them. In 1963 Zampi passed away unexpectedly, and La Romanella was put up for sale. A Jewish businessman, Peter Boizot, had realized that pizza had commercial potential during a period he'd spent in Italy, so he acquired La Romanella and opened Pizza Express in 1966. Mario Molino tells the story of how one day he was walking along Wardour Street when he saw a sign-painter on a ladder painting on the wall the letters *Pizz*…: "The painter was Peter Boizot, who told me he was opening a pizzeria and asked me who I was. 'I'm from Naples,' I answered, 'and I know how to make pizza.' This is how I started to work for Boizot." At the height of its expansion, Pizza Express had hundreds of restaurants across the whole of the UK. In 1993 John Metcalf, the wine buyer, decided to include Prosecco on the wine list. Pizza

Express was the first large chain to sell the wine, and at a time when Prosecco sales were still small. Boizot sold the chain in 2003.

The paladins of Prosecco

"I've always had a fondness for capable people who don't show off their capacities. Their gaze is often gentle and profound, and they are full of wisdom – they remind me of my father Giuseppe. Over the years such people have become my friends. I hope that their gentleness of spirit is not overcome by the aggressive attitudes of those who like to show their power and superiority. This wouldn't be a danger if each of us reflected more of our real worth. This is something society too readily denies, in attributing all merit to individuals rather than to a combination of more or less chance circumstances." (Lorenzo Zonin)

Enzo Di Nolfi and Franco Merloni

Originally from Avellino, Enzo Di Nolfi, the owner of the Raffaella restaurant in Ashford, left Italy in the 1970s. He was enthusiastic about the welcome he found in his adopted country; he thought all migrants should thank the Brits for the kindness they showed towards them: "We are free to express ourselves; the British are open to our culture and value our work." Enzo showed the same enthusiasm for Prosecco and made sure his restaurant was supportive in promoting it among their customers and other restaurateurs. On Sundays, when the restaurant was closed, he would bring Prosecco and grappa home to enjoy with his family and friends.

The manager of Raffaella, Franco Merloni,* used to pick porcini mushrooms in the Surrey woods and give them to Antonio Carluccio, who at the time used to go and eat in the San Domenico restaurant in Cobham. Franco, whenever he was drunk, would rail against priests, because of a nasty experience in his youth. Then he found out that his wife was having an affair with his best friend, but he forgave his friend and grew even fonder of him when he saw how upset he was because he'd done wrong. The police back in Pianello del Lario, the village on the shore of Lake Como where he had been born, were searching for him for cigarette and petrol smuggling. Franco left his wife and took off. He never found peace and equilibrium in England, but he is remembered fondly by those who knew him.

Roberto Gardetto

Piedmont is one of the most industrialized parts of Italy, and there has been less migration in the restaurant business in this region than in others. Roby, a former professional photographer from the Val di Susa, came to England to learn the language. This is how he tells his story:

"I went to school with my friend Vanni; for eight years we'd go back to his house to have our snacks. Sometimes he came to visit me at home, and then in the evening, especially at the weekend, we would go to the bar of Renzo "Paluc" and eat one of his delicious ice creams... You'd then go into another room, like a long dark corridor, with a black-and-white television, one of the very few TV sets in the whole village, and we'd watch the quiz programme 'Double or Quits'. There was a row of about twenty chairs, and the smoke was so thick you could have cut it with a knife... Dear Lord, how many years ago was all that? Sundays I went to church, and I was there all day, as I was an altar boy; Don Bonaudo would give us hot chocolate and biscuits to keep us happy; there were two masses in the morning and another in the evening... Anyway, it was all this which made me realize I needed to do something if I was going to get anywhere in life. I left Italy in 1979 and went to Windsor, about thirty kilometres from London. Next to Windsor there's Eton, with its famous school. I made up my mind to stay here and learn English. After a year, I decided to find work in one of the hotel restaurants near Heathrow airport, where wealthy Arabs went to eat. In those days, restaurants had French staff in the kitchen to do the cooking and Italian staff in the dining room. French food was better known and sophisticated, while Italian waiters were friendly and welcoming. After a couple of years spent doing this, along with the chef Toni Zizza, I decided to try for upmarket restaurants. In order to improve my French I went to France and worked for the fashion designer Pierre Gardin, who was originally from Treviso. I used to spend the winters in Paris and the summers in Cannes. Then, because I wanted to be with my girlfriend Lynne, I returned to England and opened a restaurant, Il Cambio, in a fifteenth-century building in Guilford. There was a long narrow and very steep staircase that led to the dining room; the waiters needed to be agile. The room itself was irregularly shaped, and it had low wooden beams, so diners had to be careful not to bang their heads. Business was slow to begin with, because of the Falklands War; the real upturn, when it came, was due to the support of the chef Silvano Mazzoli, a young man from Reggio Emilia. The success encouraged us, and we decided to take on a new challenge. Together with Lorenzo Castiglioni we opened the new Cambio – it was elegant and modern. That was sold in 2007, at the peak of its success.* Regrets? None whatsoever. It's emotions that count, and my life has been full of those." Roberto was an admirer of Piedmontese wines, and for him the only sparkling wine was champagne. So he was dubious at first about Prosecco, but afterwards, thanks to his business partner Lorenzo, he started to appreciate the Veneto and Prosecco.

Carlo Cataldi

"I'm from Fiuggi" was how Carlo Cataldi introduced himself to Fabio Terrinoni, the owner of the Villa D'Este restaurant in Marlow. "I'm from Fiuggi too," replied Fabio.

"Everyone in Fiuggi knew my father, because he was the road sweeper," added Carlo. "Then your father must have known my father, since he worked as a plumber for the municipality," replied Fabio. "Everyone in Fiuggi knew my father, because he was always drunk – and when he came home, he would beat me." "Then he must have known my father, since he was always drunk too." Carlo's difficult family background didn't prevent him from tackling life fearlessly, in Fiuggi, a town not short of dangerous individuals. One day, someone came into his restaurant armed with heavy chains. Carlo, who's of middling height and average build, without a moment's hesitation leapt over the bar and threw himself on the man, grabbing him from behind and by the neck and clasping his legs around his body. He let go when the brute lost his balance and fell down. The diners thought they were watching a scene from a comedy film. Carlo's proud of his bravery: "I can deal with crazy people, because as soon as I lock eyes with them they realize they're dealing with someone who's crazier than they are." This theory has always worked, except once, when three thugs, without so much as even looking at him, hit him from behind so forcefully he had to go to hospital, bleeding and unrecognizable. Having an alcoholic father was an incentive for Carlo to make his own way in the world. He was creative, and together with Giorgio Collazzo and Angelo Camassa opened Il Lizardo in Fulham. Camassa recalls that "Carlo, always full of invention, just used the new restaurant to experiment with his design skills". Casa Carlo replaced the old name Il Lizardo, and every six months Carlo would redesign the space. Casa Carlo became a second home for young Italians who needed some support and encouragement. Carlo was always happy to help Italians who found themselves in difficulty. Prosecco needed a lift up too, and Carlo helped to promote it after 1989. He went into partnership with a famous former footballer who had drinking problems; thanks to this relationship the word Prosecco kept being mentioned in articles in the *Independent, The Times* and the *Evening Standard*, as well as gaining a couple of TV appearances. Later Carlo opened a new Casa Carlo on the New King's Road. He succeeded in turning the old public lavatories into a delightful small restaurant,* which he was constantly redecorating.

Among the habitués of Casa Carlo there was an eccentric fantasist by the name of Piero, originally from Puglia. He told people he worked as a trader on the floor of the London Stock Exchange. All the young migrants in Casa Carlo, anxious to succeed, used to listen to his stories, because Piero seemed to offer some hope of what they might too become. Between glasses of Prosecco, he would tell them in elaborate detail about his exotic travels and how wealthy he was. He took everyone in for months, so much so that someone in financial difficulties even asked him for a loan. "No problem" replied Piero, "I'll help you out." But from that day on he wasn't seen again. Later it was discovered that he worked as a porter at the Halkin Hotel, a luxury hotel near Belgrave Square. Piero simply absorbed other people's stories, appropriating the experiences of the hotel's clientele.

Angelo Camassa, known as Charlie

Angelo, from Ostuni in Puglia, left Italy at the end of the 1970s. He came to London and first earned a living by dressing as Charlie Chaplin and letting tourists photograph him with them. Since then, everyone called him "Charlie" or "Charlino". Charlie's life has been dominated by his passion for roulette and blackjack. He started to frequent gaming houses when he was working at Pizza Pucci. "Chronic gamblers are just losers" – so says Lino della Pesca, an ex-croupier. And Charlie's earnings soon evaporated. One day Charlie decided to abandon his job as a maître d' and devote himself to gambling. He told his friends he'd worked out a system for winning and went off to Malaga to spend his time doing what he most enjoyed: gambling. He flew to Malaga airport and took a taxi to the hotel. About a kilometre before reaching his destination, he saw a casino. So as soon as he got to the hotel, he told the taxi to wait, handed his bags to a porter and went back to the casino he'd just spotted. He gambled, won, lost, won again, lost again and finally – three hours after landing at Malaga airport – lost all his money. He didn't even have the money to pay for a sandwich. He returned to the hotel, where he assured the manager that friends in London would send him all the money he needed. He met with some sympathy and understanding in the hotel from people who'd had the same problems. He phoned Maurizio Selci of the pizzeria L'Artista in Golders Green, who agreed to transfer enough money for him to settle his hotel bill and pay for a return flight. After waiting some days for the money to arrive, when it did, instead of flying back to London, Charlie headed back to the casino. Here he won more than he'd lost the previous time, then lost some of it, then won even more, and then at the end lost everything again. An old lady who saw his dejection offered him some money, which immediately went up in smoke too. However, Charlie always found the solution, in the end, to such ups and downs. In 1994, with financial help from his friend Teo Catino, he opened his own restaurant, Charlie's Pizza, in Hornsey, a neighbourhood where only Charlie would have thought of starting a business. It was a success, and afterwards, with his girlfriend Sara, he opened a second restaurant in Enfield. Years later, when everything seemed to be steaming ahead just fine, Charlie started going to casinos again. In a short space of time he lost the two restaurants – as well as his girlfriend. He asked for help from Teo, who told him he'd already given him a step up once before. It didn't matter – Charlie is a proud spirit, and he's endlessly resourceful. Gambling for him is a way of putting yourself constantly on the line; there's an unconscious desire to dismiss what other people take so seriously, an inability to really regard as important the objectives you've set out. He's always attracted a circle of friends and acquaintances around him, and glasses of

Prosecco have always accompanied his socializing. Up to 2013 he managed Charlie's Pizza in Golders Green, where he used to play the guitar to welcome customers.

Paolo Mancassola

In Verona, Paolo was a butcher. "When I was eleven, I'd go after school to practise in the local butcher's shop. When I finished high school, I was already working there full-time." In 1981, when he was twenty, Paolo decided to spend three months in London, on holiday but occasionally working to support himself. As a trained butcher, various restaurant kitchens appreciated his skills, and he worked as a meat chef. He put off returning to Italy and changed jobs frequently; he wasn't looking for a permanent set-up, and didn't want to settle. He met Maha, his future wife, and accepted the offer to manage the Valentino restaurant on the Edgware Road. His fondness for Prosecco dated back to the day when his father Umberto would go to Valdobbiadene to buy direct from the wine producers. He also used to drink grappa when he went skiing in the winter, to keep warm. The memory of the way Prosecco was poured into a carafe in order to filter out the bottle's sediments gave Paolo an idea of how to present the wine to British diners. He'd told the sales rep that he'd included Prosecco in the restaurant's wine list, but had only succeeded in selling one crate of bottles in a year. The rep showed him the carafe, which could then be placed in the ice bucket, and Paolo remembered how it was done back at home. "This 'gimmick' was a game-changer – it meant that now there was a little story to tell about the wine." Once he'd found the technique, Paolo's enthusiasm knew no bounds. He was also keen to promote grappa, but thought that it was an acquired taste. He went on offering it to customers, until they grew to like it and became grappa addicts, and he also converted his friends, who then started to order bottles for their own consumption.*

Doriano Castellani*

Doriano comes from a family of hoteliers in Vicenza. His grandfather on his father's side was a Fascist mayor, an old braggart who would sit down to eat in a trattoria and use the old thousand-lira banknote as a tablecloth. His other grandfather, Francesco – his mother's father – was an anti-Fascist. Once, in wartime, during a Fascist parade, with Mussolini present, a young militant smacked Francesco in the face, because he hadn't taken off his hat when Il Duce appeared. "You're a bully here in front of all your comrades," Doriano's grandfather told the youngster, "but just come and see me at home and I'll give you what for." Some days later, the young Fascist did visit Francesco and was shot dead. They buried him by a large oak tree near the spot where he was killed. Once the war was over, Doriano's grandfather told the police what had happened. As for the other grandfather, the Fascist mayor, the partisans took care of him. Doriano is full of true stories like this one, old and new, infused with an uncommon sense of morality, always fascinating to listen to. He would tell the story of an Italian migrant who sold hosiery as a street trade and never missed an opportunity to pull one over his customers. On one occasion, he managed to sell twenty-three pairs of shoes to a chef who worked at the Il Falconiere restaurant on Old Brompton Road; once he'd taken them home, the purchaser realized all the pairs were missing a shoe. This shady erstwhile street trader is now a famous chef and has published cookery books. The courage to leave their country has given some Italians the opportunity to acquire notoriety; what were limitations of character become virtues in their adopted country.

Gino Ruocco

"The prettiest wild flowers grow on the poorest soil."
(Geoff Hayward)*

Gino was a restaurateur and salesman originally from Minori on the Amalfi coast. He gave a lot of his time to promoting Italian wines, including Prosecco. He died in 2000 while still young.* His British clients were so fond of him that two of them offered to pay for his funeral. He was always willing to help, sometimes driving 200 kilometres to deliver a dozen bottles of Prosecco. This created a lot of publicity for the wine – but not much money to show for his efforts. Doriano, who was a friend of his, described him as "large-hearted". Gino used to describe wines as if they were people and vice versa. "Good wines depend completely on how you look after the vines. Vines do best in poor soil, rocky and marly, on a hill slope. If you grow vines in easy fertile soil you get lots of grapes to harvest, but the quality is not particularly good. The wine will lack acidity, which is essential for the body, and won't age. If vines grow in arid soil away from sunlight, then the wine will be sharp, difficult to blend. That's like spoilt people who've grown up surrounded by compliments and without hardships – they will lack the acidity which would give their character structure and, as they get older, make them interesting. On the other hand, a person who's had too many negative experiences will be too acidic: no oak barrel will ever temper and soften his or her character." Wine, like people, can get better with age, but improvements are the result of certain conditions.*

Antonio Melina

Antonio started to work as a mechanic when he was nine years old in the province of Catanzaro, where he was born. When he was fifteen, his father died, so he had to work to support his five younger siblings. At sixteen he moved to Turin and went to work at the Fiat car factory. In 1968, when he was eighteen, he moved to England, when he learnt that Rolls-Royce was looking to recruit Italian mechanics. While he was working for Rolls-Royce, he grew to appreciate British politeness, but also suffered from the prejudices of his fellow car-workers. After ten years as a car-worker, he had to change job, because his back was giving him trouble. His doctor said he'd started to work at too young an age. So he found a new job in a coffee bar, where he met his future wife Rosetta. She was the daughter of the owners of the bar, who were, like Antonio, from Calabria. His new in-laws had come to England in the 1950s to work in the steelworks in Sheffield. Then they changed jobs and started to work in a steakhouse and afterwards opened their own coffee bar, which also sold Italian products like pasta and cheese.

Before he set up his own distributing company for Italian food and wine, Antonio worked as a sales rep for Annessa Imports. That was when he became interested in selling Prosecco. When he set up his own business, as a sideline he repaired espresso machines. Following a couple of unfortunate business experiences with badly chosen partners, he had to sell his house and go back to renting somewhere to live. Now that he is nearly seventy he complains: "I've made so many mistakes, putting my trust in everyone, and yet I still haven't learnt: I make the same errors. Fortune has sometimes pointed the way, but I was never clever enough to seize the opportunity. I suppose I'm destined to have to work all my life." Despite these negative experiences, Toni continues to fight on, working from dawn till dusk, and at weekends. One of his friends, Francesco Maschio, a young man who's come to London to put to good use his degree in economics, really admires him: "Toni has great qualities of friendliness and spontaneity, which endear him to everyone. That's no small achievement."

PART FOUR

New social trends

Giovanni Di Iulio from Molise has said: "Once we had to struggle to inform clients about our food and get them to taste authentic dishes. Now people think they know a lot about it, and they think they know more than we do." Over the last two decades, a wide variety of Italian food products have become available in the UK, and the quality has improved. Mario Arricale, of the Bufi restaurant in Finchley, puts this down to more frequent trips to Italy thanks to low-cost flights: "The British visit Italy and try out new dishes and wines while they're there. When they get back home, they want to find the same products here." The sales rep Gian Piero Gorietti, from Foligno in Umbria, remarked as early as 1990: "In Umbria you can find Prosecco everywhere. That means it's become an Italian product, not just a regional one, and as such people expect to find it on the wine list of any Italian restaurant." Prosecco was already popular throughout Italy, Germany and Switzerland, and the way the various international markets work together made it inevitable it would make its way into the UK. Di Iulio himself, the former owner of Casa Giovanni on Finchley Road, was encouraged by Massimo Mastrangelo, owner of the Villa Livia in Termoli, who recommended him to try Prosecco: "If Massimo buys it, then I should have it too." Rod and

Sue Ganner, who live in Manchester, got to know and like Prosecco when they were staying with friends in Tuscany, and in the 1990s took to ordering supplies directly from Italy, which they would then share with their neighbours.

After the Mionetto family ceased to be active in the market, numerous other producers of Prosecco visited the UK to participate in wine trade fairs, which was then the main way of getting a foothold in a foreign market. The consortium of Prosecco producers from Conegliano and Valdobbiadene set up a series of presentations at the prestigious Institute of Directors in London, providing the possibility for an ever-increasing number of wine producers to show their wines and organize tastings. In this way, small and medium-sized producers were helped to find distributors. The trade fairs in the sector, notably the London Wine Fair and Vinitaly* in Verona, played a fundamental role. The increase in production encouraged winemakers to find new markets abroad. All of them won more space in the market as the image of Italian food improved and the international restaurant business increasingly took Italian products on board. The circumstances were favourable, and young managers and chefs started to think about starting up their own restaurants; for every restaurant that closed down, three new ones would open up. While some of the suppliers made a loss because their clients went bankrupt, new and advantageous prospects emerged for others. All the Italian distributors proposed at least one brand of Prosecco.

Over the course of this development, other wine producers came to the fore in the regions of Valdobbiadene and Conegliano, such as Val D'Oca,* Bortolomiol, Foss Marai, Belussi, Col Vetoraz, Primo Franco, Adami, Canevel, Malibràn, Bellenda, Merotto and others. The producers were in close contact with the sommeliers working in the restaurants; a glass of Prosecco became a standard way of welcoming diners in many restaurants. Sales of the wine by the glass were continually increasing. This encouraged a higher demand for the bubblier spumante than for the less sparkling *frizzante*. Newspapers and specialist magazines devoted more column inches to Prosecco, now at the height of its success in Italy. Exports went on rising; the consumer data today is a clear indication of Prosecco's success.*

Supermarkets

As its reputation grew, so other retail sectors became interested in Prosecco. It started to appear on supermarket shelves from about 2005, a confirmation that the wine had now really arrived on the scene.*

> *"The retail wine trade in the UK is difficult because supermarkets control consumption by means of promotional offers. The abundance of promotional offers diminishes the value and the image of the wine being sold."* (Gianni Segatta)

Italo and Laura Cuccato observed, during a short trip to Britain, that "some UK supermarkets display low-quality products, especially fruit and vegetables. The appetizing smells you get in the fruit-and-veg section in an Italian supermarket are missing, because so much has to be imported and loses its freshness and aroma by the time it's displayed." In 2013 the Master of Wine* Christopher Burr, together with a team of expert tasters, carried out an in-depth survey of the wines on offer in the main supermarket chains. After tasting 4,000 different wines, they reported their conclusions: "Sixty-eight per cent of the wine sold is undrinkable and shows evident flaws in its production. Some are quite filthy, badly produced, with excessive acidity, or adulterated, or too sugary. Others have a sameness about them – they are woody, dull, without any of the specific characteristics which link a wine to a particular vineyard or *territoire*." The quality of the wine on offer in the supermarkets depends on two factors: consumer demand for low-cost food products and the speculation of suppliers. British people tend to cut expenditure on food rather than, say, new gadgets. Some supermarkets promote food products using various techniques, including the endorsement of celebrity chefs.* The implicit message is to highlight the cook who can transform cheap ingredients into appetizing dishes. The bottles of wine found on supermarket shelves have, with very few exceptions, tailor-made labels: producers are not even mentioned. Profiting from the popularity of Prosecco, large bottling firms far away from the zones of actual production are part of the business; more savvy consumers go to look for their wine in small food retail outlets or specialist wine shops. In Italy, by contrast, ordinary people are aware of quality, and you can find the most prestigious Prosecco producers on supermarket shelves.

Irregularities in the market

A globalized market favours easy consumption, but that can also give rise to corners being cut and rules being flouted. It's in this context that the phenomenon of illicit trade in wine occurs, made even more appealing to fraudsters by the high level of excise duties. This illicit, tax-avoiding trade in wines and spumanti is widespread in the UK. Various commercial operators right across the country have denounced the presence of clandestine alcoholic beverages. The situation should be of concern to legitimate producers, since wines of illegal provenance and dubious quality have Italian names on the labels. Sean Jarvis, in charge of buying at the St Austell Brewery in Cornwall, has noted that most of the wine illegally sold is Italian, not French or Spanish. Some off-licences and dishonest restaurants sell well-known Italian wines for which the name of the producer is untraceable. Both the UK and Italian tax authorities are ineffective in tracking down the people who are cheating the system, and their failure risks damaging the genuine efforts of many people who work in the sector.

There are also those who counterfeit wine. Working in unhygienic conditions, untrained wine producers both make and distribute wine to restaurants. Franco Rimonti recalls how, in the 1980s, he used to make wine in the cellar of a building in Newcastle: "I obtained the concentrate through the manager of a distributor of Italian food. During the night I heated huge pots to boil up the ingredients: water, sucrose, grape concentrate, plus – my personal touch – lots of rosemary. My wife Sheila and my daughter Francesca would buy the large quantities of sugar needed in different shops around the city to avoid arousing suspicion. What you got was a reddish beverage, 14 degrees proof, which we called 'barberone'. Customers would queue up to reserve a bottle. I later fell out with my business partner, because too much 'easy' money was going around, and I stopped production despite the restaurateurs' insistence I continue." But Franco, always recognizable in the black hat he wore all the time, later became an active and well-liked promoter and distributor of quality Italian wines in the North-East. When he reached retirement age, he went back with his wife to his native city of Latina to enjoy his garden and the sea. At first he thought he'd be able to settle back easily into Italian life, but after a couple of years he returned to Newcastle for a short period, before going back again to Italy and finally settling in Portugal.

English wines*

The question is still out on whether it's possible to produce good wine in southern England. Lack of sunshine and frequent rain are not advantageous conditions for vineyards. Climate change – probably a result of global warming – with hotter summers has encouraged new producers to try. The use of new technologies and the addition of sugars can produce wines and sparkling wines which are quite pleasant to drink. The British like to think of themselves producing good wine, and encourage new producers to take on the challenge. While they wait for the climate to become more favourable towards their aspirations, there have always been some Italians who make wine by importing the grapes directly from Italy. In Maidenhead, Rosario Sardo, who runs the Italian Continental Store, is one of them: each year he buys containers of grapes to make wine for his customers. Similarly, Giuliano Binanti, from Jesi, the owner of Giuliano's in Edinburgh, has a cellar in his house equipped with small barrels, a press and other tools for filtering the must. His parents were agricultural workers, and as a small boy he used to help his dad make wine. He produces a white wine with a flavour of bananas and a herby red which is very good as an accompaniment to roast Scottish partridges and woodcocks.

The restaurateur Peter Bagatti, the owner of Bagatti's in Croydon, associates the wine his uncles used to make with hunting. "Many years ago, my uncle Pino Oriani used to import grapes. We children would trample the fruit with our bare feet until all the juice ran out. It was autumn, the hunting season. My other uncle, Andrea, introduced me both to wine and to hunting – he taught me how to fire a gun when I was twelve. We would leave at five in the morning; we'd have breakfast – a bread roll with mortadella, a glass of Lambrusco – and then we'd begin to shoot. A couple of times I fell asleep still holding the gun. We shot pheasants, rabbits and hares – foxes too. We'd cut their brushes off and present them to the landowner, who was happy to let us hunt on his land. Not all my uncle's hunting companions were good shots. Once we went out shooting, and one of the hunters fired his gun by mistake. Some of the shot hit me in the calf – you can still see the scars today. But no fuss was made. We bound a handkerchief round the wound, and only when the hunt was over was I taken to a hospital to receive treatment. One day I shot at a rabbit, which managed to hide itself in its burrow. It probably died. Since then I've never hunted."

The UK today

"Where are the gentlemen?" (Marcello Gobbi)

According to a poll published at the beginning of 2013, about 45% of London residents are white British. The figure is even lower if you consider that many EU citizens living in the UK are not registered, and that a number of illegal immigrants from outside the EU are not included. The flow of foreigners into the UK is constantly increasing because the country offers the possibility of integration to all, is tolerant towards people of different races and sees itself as a social arena where individual qualities such as determination, imagination and creativity find expression. If the early immigrants did the work the British disdained to do, then the children of those immigrants today are free to study, become doctors, lawyers or bankers, while the new Italians who come to live in London today have nothing in common with their impoverished precursors, but are well educated and looking forward to brilliant careers. The Sicilian Filippo Mangione is a graduate of the Bocconi University in Milan and worked in the USA and in Italy before coming to London "to make", as he says, "all the money my parents spent on my education worthwhile".

The UK receives a vast flow of foreign investment, which allows the country to prosper beyond its actual potential. Foreign entrepreneurs buy up factories, hotel chains, famous department stores, and encourage the importation of products and ways of life from their home countries.

The architecture has also undergone changes. In city centres, new buildings can be put up next to old edifices. Architects from other nations and cultures who want to make their mark find the right opportunities in London, which as a city is intent on blending the past and the present, the traditional and the modern.

The British countryside, on the other hand, remains the same – the love and respect for nature, for woods and animals, an environmental respect which has its roots in the past, with rural areas concentrated in the hands of a few landowners who survived without needing to exploit their resources. The woodlands, with their squirrels, deer and rabbits have the atmosphere of a fairy tale (although foxes now prefer to roam urban areas at night and rummage in waste bins). On hillsides sheep, cows and horses graze, like something out of a Nativity scene, though you would be hard pushed to see a shepherd. Gabriele Nodari, who regularly goes hunting for chanterelle mushrooms and chestnuts in the British countryside, declares he has never seen anyone working in the fields.

Pietro De Cesare remarks, with an air of satisfaction, how much food and wine consumption has changed in the UK in recent years. "Who could have foreseen Italian food becoming so influential? The Italian capacity for creative thinking, combined with the efficiency of the UK Government, has profoundly shaped the British nation. Italians feel at ease here, and living in London is like being at home." Espresso coffee, though not as good as you'd find in Naples, is drunk in bars all over the country. Glasses of grappa and limoncello are routinely offered at the end of meals in Italian restaurants. Dante Diaferia notes that "you can buy panettone the whole year round, and not just at Christmas".

Michele Rinaldi, who works for Birra Moretti, also points out how popular Italian beer has become in the UK. "As with Prosecco, Italian beer became familiar thanks to Italian restaurateurs and distributors. In the 1970s and 1980s, the first importers were Ciborio, Carnevale and Continental Wine & Food, but it was an uphill struggle, given that the UK is one of Europe's leading countries for the production and consumption of beer. Italian beer became popular only after wine did. Up to a few years ago most British people didn't even know Italy had beer, despite the fact we've got a long tradition of beer-making, with the two leading brands, Moretti and Peroni, dating back to the mid-nineteenth century. When I first started out in the business, I remember taking some bottles of beer to a British client, who looked at me in surprise as he put the bottles on the table. "Do you really believe anyone here is going to start drinking Italian beer?" he asked me incredulously. Six years later, sales of Moretti have tripled. Peroni is actually the bottled beer with the highest sales in the UK, outstripping even British beers, with a consumption of more than 900,000 hectolitres a year. Carlsberg are promoting their Italian beer, Poretti, while Menabrea has recently signed a commercial agreement in Scotland with C&C, the owners of Tennent's, the leading brand in Scotland. Interest in Italian beer is growing, and it isn't confined just to the well-known brands. In fashionable pubs in London you can find Italian beers from small producers.

So Italian beer is definitely on the up in the UK. It took a bit longer than Prosecco, but now it's really becoming successful. In future I can see a growth of interest in Italian craft beers."

So the Italianization of food in the UK has been achieved. The Italians resident in the UK remain a vital point of reference for the large export companies, whereas medium and smaller-scale producers still encounter difficulties. Nowadays you can find many Italian wines in the UK, but it's still a remarkable fact that since 2014 Prosecco had the highest sales of any sparkling wine in the country in terms of bottles sold, outstripping champagne* and cava. Prosecco is a wine you can drink on a daily basis, while at the same time champagne has lost its aura of exclusivity, meaning wine snobs have to seek out the more recherché labels to maintain their sense of superiority. Some operators in the sector have damaged the interests of champagne by revealing the methods used in its production, demythologizing it in the process and stripping it of its mystery. Even Attilio Mionetto, who drew inspiration from the French model of champagne promotion, wistfully remarks: "Champagne was a dream; now it's just another wine."

Prosecco in the UK is now here to stay; you can find it in international restaurants, clubs, supermarkets, hospitals, hairdressing salons, hotels and universities.* It's just another part of what the British eat and drink.

The restaurant business

Recently the Italian restaurant business in the UK has shown
signs of change, and it seems likely it will go on changing.
Many restaurants are empty; they close and then reopen
and then shut down again, leaving suppliers and the tax
authorities to pick up the bills. But they are still hanging in
there, often because the Italian staff don't have other jobs
to go to. The reasons for the crisis were predictable. Italian
dishes are now found everywhere on the menus of restaurants offering international cooking; even Alain Ducasse at
the Dorchester Hotel puts pasta on the menu. Then there is
a growing number of so called "gastropubs", which offer a
menu of international dishes with Italian influences, made
by chefs from various countries. The increased competition has cut down on profits, while the cost of rent and raw
materials makes the future uncertain. Restaurants in the
centres of cities and towns do well because urban people
don't want to travel long distances. Celebrity chefs can use
TV appearances and shows to publicize their ever-increasing
restaurant chains in a way that is quite impossible for ordinary restaurants. Restaurant chains proliferate, rationaliz-
ing costs and staff. For all these reasons, the growth of the
Italian restaurant trade is slowing down; some young Italian
chefs now prefer to work in prestigious but non-Italian

restaurants. Likewise, many young Italians are only prepared to work as waiters temporarily, unlike the Italians after the war, who saw the profession of being a waiter as a satisfying one. Roberto Simeone makes the accusation that "many Italians have gone into the wrong profession: the restaurant business is just a makeshift for them; they lack passion and dedication, they don't realize they're working in the most important industry of all: the hospitality industry".

> *"There are young people today who think waiting at table is humiliating. They take no pleasure in their work – and that's a sure way of never getting promoted. But there are some really excellent young people too – only that they are scared to take the risk of setting up their own businesses."*
> (Giuseppe Cipriani)*

Even the "Italianness" of Italian food is on the wane, watered down by individual chefs' subjective interpretations of dishes: it's losing its character. "There's a lot of confusion," admits Francesco Mazzei of the restaurant Anima in the City of London. Francesco is a young chef who, despite his success, tries hard to lead a normal life (he points out proudly that he always takes his kids to school in the morning). Gino Taddei also confesses his state of uncertainty: "I don't know what Italian cooking is any more. When I opened Cibo in 1989, I was inspired by regional cooking, with all its traditional dishes and ways of doing things. Now you get personality chefs who use the old names for their own inventions. But why don't they just give them new names?" The chef Roberto Peruzzo, who is working hard to cultivate a taste for Italian food in the little town of Alnwick, with three restaurants near the castle where the Harry Potter films were shot, was taken aback on learning that a French chef was giving lessons on Italian cooking: "He thought you could make Genoese pesto without basil." Restaurant chains are run by foreign businessmen who want to exploit the fashion for "Made in Italy" and are motivated entirely by profit. There are lots of Italian restaurants owned by Turks, Iranians, Portuguese and Albanians. Andrea Riva mentions certain famous Italian restaurants run by British people – who may be good at using the media for publicity, but perhaps feel the need to combat the general perception that the British are no good at cooking.

The initial impetus and energy has died out, and the Italian restaurant business in the UK has become sluggish. Felice Mutti, who runs the Due Amici in Kent, would like to sell up, but doesn't for the simple reason that his loyal staff, now in their sixties, wouldn't find another job if he did. Antonio Trapani, of the Montpeliano restaurant in Knightsbridge, knows that after forty successful years he should make a change and get rid of the old staff who've been with him for thirty years: "They're tired and have got nothing new to offer our customers. But it breaks my heart to send them away." It's moving to see this sense of compassion in experienced businessmen, who also know that their restaurants are slowly dying.

Juan Rio, from Spain, works in the Italian restaurant business as the owner of five restaurants. He complains that his former business partner didn't listen to him: "If he had, by now we would have thirty restaurants. Now he's still running the two restaurants he's always had; he's not proved capable of renewing himself." Some restaurateurs entrust the continuation of the business to their children, who can introduce innovative and up-to-date ideas. The Sicilian Ciro Corsaro, who owns the Made in Italy Group, has succeeded in persuading his four children – Giuseppe, Sara, Valentina and Angelo – to play a part in his long-term projects, while Rinaldo Mollura* is hopeful that his three children, with their education, will do better than he did. But most children of restaurateurs choose to follow their own paths; they're educated, often privately, and that holds out the prospect of jobs which are or at least seem to be less demanding. "My son works in the Stock Exchange and earns more than me. Now he behaves like some of my old customers," Alberto Pagano of the Cappuccetto boasts. Others exploit the wealth their parents have carefully accumulated: "I'm not a fool: I prefer to go sailing," says one, "all due respect to Mum and Dad, who've led a life of sacrifice to become millionaires. They're just workaholics, I'm sorry to say – they need to go to a rehabilitation centre, if one existed for workaholics." Other unluckier restaurateurs have dedicated all their time to their work and have lost track of their children. Others remarry and start a new family when they're older, and lose the chance of living out a quiet retirement.

New ideas

The Sicilian Enzo Oliveri, a partner in the restaurant chain Fratelli La Bufala,* is committed to preserving the image of Italian food. In 2012 he ran as a candidate for the European parliamentary elections with a campaign focused on defending Italian products. He spoke for everyone when he declared that the Italian restaurant business needs to reinvent itself. The dynamic restaurateur Domenico Taravella, who runs restaurants in the small towns of Somerset, is trying to come up with new ideas to reinvigorate old traditions, while at the same time involving the young Italians he recruits as staff for the project. One of his ideas is to do home delivery for ready-cooked Italian meals, something which up to now has only been done for pizzas. "Restaurants must be run like factories, with a focus on logistics and efficient service." Doriano Castellani, on his return from a recent trip to Italy, has found fresh ideas on how to go about things. "In Italy you find restaurants with limited menus and fewer dishes.* There's a need to recover a sense of family cooking, which we're in danger of losing because the family unit itself is getting weaker in today's society. So restaurants take over from families; the waiter offers a limited choice of dishes to customers, like 'special dishes of the day'. Italians are not prepared to accept the compromises you need to make when you eat in restaurant chains." Diners want to relax and are happy for the owner to choose what they're going to eat. "This is how I like to do things," reflects Carlo Crosta of Carlo's Trattoria when he serves up grilled seabass he fished himself; by contrast, Riccardo Guglielmini, the owner and chef at Tentazioni, has misgivings about the idea: "Customers need to feel they're having a different dining experience than they would get at home." Riccardo's view underlines a distinction between two types of clientele, which the Emilian sales rep Giacomo Balducci has summed up like this: "There are customers who eat out every day and others who just go to a restaurant for special occasions. The former – and there are many in London – want plain, healthy cooking that won't upset their digestive systems." But while the old-timers in the restaurant business are pessimistic, others are coming up with solutions for the future.

Riccardo Grigolo, Al Boccon di'vino

The Venetian Riccardo Grigolo opened Al Boccon di'vino in Richmond in 2010. There wasn't a wine list, and you couldn't choose what you wanted to eat. Riccardo didn't speak English, but managed to convey what he was thinking and feeling with looks and gestures. Customers went along without protest; if they did complain, he'd invite them to go to another restaurant – after all, there was no shortage of choice in the vicinity. On one occasion, two women were talking excitedly to him. Riccardo listened to them with a smile on his face and then turned to the neighbour-ing table: "*Cossa gae dito?*" ("What are they saying?"). A glass of Prosecco would arrive without fail at the table, like compulsory medicine. Riccardo decided to go into the restaurant business at the age of fifty-three, after working for the Italian Touring Club. He employed non-Italians in the kitchen, explaining, in 2012, why: "My two chefs come from Nepal and Bangladesh. I tried to recruit Italians, but they never listened to me or followed my instructions." Riccardo instructs his staff just like Italian mothers instruct their daughters. Today Riccardo is fluent in English, and the restaurant is well known. He offers only a few dishes, using quality ingredients in simple combinations. Simona Gilmeanu, from Romania, is the manager. It's not the kind of restaurant which would work everywhere, but it's the right formula for Richmond. Diners accept and enjoy the dishes they're given, just as they would if friends invited them round for dinner. The restaurant is very successful, and you need to book in advance to be sure of finding a table. Al Boccon di'vino offers a model for how to limit the costs of running a restaurant by offering a limited number of dishes.

Carlo Distefano and the San Carlo Group

"Fortune favours the brave" – so says Lino della Pesca when he thinks of his old friend Carlo Distefano, a Sicilian from Ragusa. The old saying doesn't take account of the cour-age of those who find themselves in difficult circumstances precisely because of their bravery. Carlo came to England in 1962 at the age of seventeen with a permit to work as a barber, the possibility of changing his job after four years and a capital of twelve pounds. His father had told him to keep something back from the twelve pounds as at home Carlo had two sisters to be married. Carlo opened his first restaurant in Birmingham in 1992 at the age of forty-seven. Two years later he started to expand, opening a San Carlo in Manchester, and then in Leicester, Bristol, London, Liverpool and Leeds – and in other cities overseas. His restaurants increase in number all the time, with the acquisition of new properties. "He's never put a foot wrong," says his friend Pietro De Cesare. Carlo's view of the matter is that "to keep the fire alight you need to keep throwing wood on it". His manager Augusto Tramontano agrees: "He is constantly doing up his restaurants. Even when they're doing well, he gives them a makeover." In an interview given to the Italian-language newspaper *Londra Sera*,* Carlo remarked that his restaurants have a turnover of more than sixty million pounds a year and employ more than a thousand staff. In his view, the reason for their success is the quality of the food: "Pachino tomatoes, aubergines and peppers from Siracusa, artichokes from Lazio and beef from Tuscany." But the real reason for his success is his own motivation, determination and stamina. "I haven't been on holiday for over ten years, except when my daughter Marisa got married," he told the paper, and went on to describe how he runs his business empire: "No email. I do business either face to face or on the telephone. I'm always in one of my restaurants; I use my chauffered Rolls-Royce as my office. The salaries of my staff are decent and guarantee their loyalty... In order to succeed in this business, you need to love good food and be a real restaurateur. Our restaurants are open even on Christmas Day, otherwise I get bored..."

The Italian North-East

*"At least politicians in the past had better table manners than those who've been our representatives over the last thirty years."**

The huge changes that have overtaken the UK in recent decades can also be seen, in different ways, in north-eastern Italy, the other area where this story of Prosecco is set.

Paolo Della Puppa left Aviano, a village in the province of Pordenone in Friuli, in the 1970s. He arrived in New York and said to himself: "This is the city where I ought to live... Where have I been until now?" But after many years in America he thinks back fondly to his youth in Aviano: "My dream is to go back and, sitting with friends, eat a piece of cheese with some salad picked from the garden, eaten straight out of the salad bowl, under the old pergola in my parents' house." But the pergola has long gone, and Paolo's memories are only that – memories. The inhabitants of the North-East have known periods of great prosperity and have become more selfish; courage and generosity have been replaced by anxiety and scorn, while the institutions of former times have been devalued. Businessmen don't have time for their families: the competitive nature of business means long hours of work and little space – and even less energy – for family ties. Like the warriors of old, the businessmen go back home to find peace and entertainment and to recharge their batteries. Their wives, who also go out to work, are tired, want attention and expect a bit of help: they often have neither the time nor the inclination to cook. "Mamma's cooking," which Lorenzo Berni spoke of with such reverence, has been replaced by the wife's cooking... who may let her family go without food if she's in a bad mood. In the general climate of prosperity, the system cannot ensure the continuity of traditional food culture, which parents once passed down to their children, and Italians are learning new habits. The changes are caused by globalization. Now there are McDonald's – the symbols of fast and standardized food – throughout the Veneto; they're not frequented only by African and Asian immigrants, ill at ease in a country which is incapable of harnessing the energy of the foreigners who come to live there, but also by young Italians who know less and less about their own gastronomy and its traditions.

Changes can also be seen in the countryside of the Veneto, due to rampant property speculation. The authorities have been giving free rein to individuals who show a lack of respect for the environment, resulting in an urban development uncontrolled and unrestricted by rules. "Who'd go back to live in Italy?" asked Gabriele Nodari as he gazes at a grey area of the countryside round Padua covered over with concrete and asphalt. As far as he's concerned, the myth of the "Bel Paese" needs to be reassessed: "There's no comparison between the Po Valley and the beauty of the British countryside." Gabriele, a wine promoter, is from Milan and left Lombardy some years ago. At the age of fifty-five he went to live in the New Forest, with horses and pigs running wild and porcini mushrooms growing between the beech trees. His ninety-year-old father Elia would like to come over and visit him, but Gabriele won't allow him to: "He's an old poacher – if he came over here to the New Forest, he'd start setting traps to catch quails and pheasants, and the authorities would arrest him and send him to jail." In recent times there's been an increase in the number of young people from the Veneto coming over to the UK to find a job, because the economy in Italy penalizes manufacturing industries and artisan trades. "Every now and then I remember why I left Italy. The system favours windbags rather than entrepreneurs" – so says Carlo Vagliasindi, a fashion retailer and the owner of Danieli, which also sells the best ice cream in Richmond. The enthusiastic attachment to one's own native country remains strong, but the unethical behaviour which has spread to every level of society makes it hard to be proud of being Italian.

"In periods of crisis, when the wind blows hard, the tree that wants to remain standing plunges its roots down into the earth; in the same way, people must cling to the old traditions..." (Gianni Zonin)

There were idealists who dreamt of a different future: less wealth, more leisure, fewer industrial complexes and more land given over to agriculture; farms looking like they used to in the past, with their porticoed buildings open to the fields, and the land given over to the cultivation of traditional crops; a flourishing hospitality industry, with more hotels and restaurants, and people trained to give a proper welcome to visitors and tourists – something Italians show a natural instinct for. Tourism then wouldn't suffer from the competition of other industrialized countries; on the contrary, it would benefit from them. Human capacities would find better expression than they can in the repetitive and alienating environment of factory work. The Po Valley would be a good place to live in, and its inhabitants more humane and sociable. Treviso would become again what it once was for Venice, and the whole world would be its client...

Going back to Italy

For young Italian migrants in the UK the prospect of ever returning to Italy is remote. The sales rep Gianluca D'Agostino feels so much at home in south-east England that while he's happy to go back to his native city Naples, it's only for holidays; he doesn't see a future for himself in Italy. Roberto Scalzo,* of Scalzo on Elizabeth Street in London, was born in England to Italian parents; when asked if he feels more Italian or British he replies: "At times it's more convenient to feel Italian, and at other times British." Pietro De Cesare argues that "the Brits have welcomed the Italians: they've given them the kind of welcome you give to people who are vulnerable but show good qualities. The Italians who don't like being in Britain should just go back to Italy." Few Italians return to the villages and towns where they were born and grew up. Antonio Crolla and Giuseppe Marini, born in Scotland to parents who came from Picinisco near Frosinone in Lazio, spend the summer and winter holidays in the village which their grandparents and parents left so long ago. Some of them have their Ferraris parked outside the local bar to show how far they've come in their lives. Other Italians who miss the sun in the UK arrange to spend their retirement in warmer climes. Many of the immigrants who came over to the UK in the 1960s and 1970s have bought houses in countries like Spain. Roberto Ballerini, Iginio Santin, Angelo Saro and Walter Mariti all live in Marbella, on the Costa del Sol. Giorgio Giusto has recently sold the Café Montpeliano and is thinking of moving to Spain; the idea of going back to Italy doesn't appeal to him. Alberto Pagano on the other hand doesn't share this negative attitude towards Italy: he built himself a villa in Pontremoli, in the Tuscan province of Massa-Carrara, and is happy to spend half of the year there and half in the UK. His beautiful house is set in the hills among olive groves, but it's also a magnet for burglars. At the beginning of 2013 Alberto was attacked by three masked robbers, who first stunned him with a blow to the face and then brought him round while holding a knife pressed to his throat. They wanted him to tell them the combination for the small wall safe they'd seen. Alberto couldn't remember it – the safe wasn't used – and managed to save himself by offering his attackers the cash he luckily had in his pockets. After that attack, he arranged to get the house protected with a system of external alarms and twelve cameras which switch on at the slightest movement, as well as reinforced windows. But his wife still gets upset every so often in the night when a prowling cat sets off the alarm.

Lino Della Pesca tells a story about his friend Mimmo Peretti, who arrived in the UK in the 1960s to work first as a chef and then as a restaurateur. In retirement, Peretti went to live in Castiglione di Ravenna: a few days after he'd left, he called Lino to tell him how happy he felt: "For the first time in my life I feel content: I've bought a little house in this beautiful village, and I've got everything I need within walking distance – the bar where I go to have a chat, the newsagent, the church and the cemetery. I've made friends with the local priest, the police officer and the barber." A month later, Peretti called Lino again, this time in a very different mood: "Oh, these Italians are real bastards! I had to pay 4,000 euros to the notary for the house purchase, when in Britain it would have cost me just £560. I asked for planning permission to build an extension so that my kids would have somewhere to stay when they come over; the council asked me to pay 6,300 euros just to hand in the application." Lino likes to collect stories about Italians. He's convinced that his friends Peretti and Rimonti will eventually come back to the UK. He himself owns a small house in the Abruzzo and knows what the problems can be. He'd promised his sister Giuseppina, who was seriously ill, to build a small chapel of rest in the cemetery of Pescina, a village near L'Aquila. He had to pay 16,000 euros to the local council to buy the few square metres of land needed, and then the builders asked for an advance of 20,000 euros on the total cost of 68,000 euros before beginning the work – all without invoices or receipts.

Many Italians remain attached to Italy, of course, at least for their holidays. Pasquale Cannarile comes from Alberobello in Puglia and is the sales manager for Alivini in the Leeds area; he says: "One day I'll go back to Puglia, because I'm fond of my village. I'm planning to build myself a house there. But I'd never go and live in a *trullo* – I was born in one, for me it's a reminder of being poor."

The future of Prosecco

"How can we stop Prosecco going the way of Pinot Grigio?" (Pietro De Cesare)

In the past the viticulture of the Veneto has undergone periods of crisis due to unforeseen circumstances not always attributable to human error. What is the future for Prosecco? Will the present fortunate trajectory continue for its producers? From as early as 2009 Prosecco has run the risk of becoming – like pizza, pasta and mozzarella – a mere name to be used and abused all over the world, with nothing to recall its link to a particular territory. It is possible to buy cans of Prosecco from Austria or Germany – and even today there are restaurants and distributors prepared to disregard the rules. For some time the sales rep Laura Pigoni has been complaining that in the UK many operating in the sector deceive customers with what they call draught or even pink Prosecco. The three Prosecco consortia* denounced the irregularities to the relevant authorities, at which point the issue was taken up and debated in the press, with some maintaining the rules didn't need to be adhered to or even claiming that the UK had the right to make its own rules. Beyond Europe, commercial irregularities are even more frequent. In California they produce a wine called Chianti which clearly has nothing to do with the region in Italy where it is actually produced, and in the wine shops of San Francisco you can find wines with names like Tocai Friulano from Oregon. It is a fact that the Italians have failed to profit as much as they could from the globalization of their own food products.

The consumption of Prosecco will continue to grow if the conditions which have enabled it to emerge and develop as a product are kept in place. Yet it's proving hard to transmit to the young the same drive which the old wine entrepreneurs in the Veneto felt towards conquering foreign markets. The circumstances which motivated older generations have changed, as the example mentioned above shows of the smug young man who preferred to go sailing and profit from his parents' hard-won wealth rather than make the sacrifices they had to make to become successful.

"You can't take on an international project if you've got a provincial cast of mind." (Luigi Bolzon)

The scornful and narrow-minded attitudes towards other Italian regions which have emerged in north-eastern Italy in recent years have undermined the sense of common belonging which Italian migrants have had in the past and which has contributed to the globalization of Prosecco. Hostility towards others is not a characteristic of the entrepreneurial class, involved in production and trade, but can be found among ordinary people and in their political choices. It may be an element in the disaffection those Italians who are resident in the UK increasingly feel towards their native country.

"Now that we've acquired farms in seven Italian regions, including Puglia and Sicily, I think my family can claim to have unified Italy." (Domenico Zonin)

The Sicilian Virgilio Gennaro* – who, together with the sommelier Loris Propedo, has included six different brands of Prosecco on the wine list of Locanda Locatelli – is disturbed by the presence of poor-quality Prosecco in the UK market. Antonio Dal Bello, who owns the eponymous winery in the Asolan hills, thinks that now that spumante is fashionable all and sundry quaff Prosecco down undiscriminatingly. The trajectory of other Italian wines justifies Alessio Fuso's* comment: "If an Italian wine ends up in the hands of the big British buyers, that's the writing on the wall for it!"

Gianni Segatta agrees: "Once they become popular, Italian wines are let down by the desire to increase quantity, without taking the consequences into consideration. I remember Lambrusco – a unique wine with a low alcohol content and very good effervescence and acidity. It disappeared because of the race to lower the price. It was red at first, then it became white and then rosé. It was eight degrees proof – and then it was zero! In the end the producers of real Lambrusco just gave up. It's the same story for Soave, Verdicchio, Frascati and now Pinot Grigio. The situation of Prosecco is worrying because, despite the fact that the local consortia have succeeded in preventing the use of the name in other countries, you can find cheap bottles in supermarkets, probably of dubious quality."

But the president of the consortium Prosecco DOCG dei Colli Asolani e del Montello, Armando Serena – a person therefore who speaks with authority – is quick to offer reassurance, explaining that controls on the production of Prosecco are extremely rigorous: "We're working hard to prevent abuses of all kinds, because we're very much aware of the problems that can arise."

Sergio De Luca too is positive. "The status of Prosecco in the UK has changed. The situation is different now. Prosecco is a whole territory, not just the gently rolling hills where I grew up. The Glera vine is cultivated across the entire Veneto plain, as far as the sea. That's benefited everyone – and the supermarkets have profited too from the upturn in production. The consumption of Prosecco has spread far and wide, to the point where your average British wine-drinker is familiar with it and also likes it in cocktails. The scale of production has increased, with the result that two typologies of Prosecco have emerged: the Prosecco which is produced in the localities where it has always, historically, been made and mass Prosecco. At present consumers in the UK can't tell the difference between the two. I look back fondly to the early pioneering days when we were struggling to get Prosecco known outside Italian restaurants, but I'm also glad that the region where

I was born has become so well known and so popular. Now as head buyer I more often find myself discussing the sale of millions of bottles of Prosecco with the giant buyers in the business than sitting in a restaurant enjoying a glass and thinking back to my youth and the marvellous region I left so many years ago."

"The Italian fashion and car industries have their leading brands. Prosecco, unlike champagne, doesn't have leading brands strong enough to safeguard its quality and identity." (Christopher Burr)

Alessandro Marchesan explains his point of view: "In the beginning, the increasing reputation of Prosecco was due to the efforts of the Mionetto family. For years they dominated the UK market and contributed to the huge success of the wine, while keeping up its good image and maintaining high prices." But Mionetto's premature withdrawal from the market, when they failed to achieve the goals they'd set themselves, left a void which has certainly benefited some but also damaged others. With no obvious market leader the market has been broken up between small or medium-scale producers and the major bottling wineries. Among the latter, there are businesses which specialize in following market trends and have no interest in a more constructive approach. So the small and medium-scale producers suffer on account of the confusion with naming, quality and price. Dalbir Singh has followed the whole saga of Prosecco from the beginning and, referring to opportunistic traders, has commented: "The companies that built up the market for Prosecco are disappearing, while in their stead some traders are emerging who will destroy it." The Italian trading class is weak: there are outstanding personalities – but also mediocre ones. The absence of any corporate structures and the lack of any system for the independent setting of prices lead to a confusion that can only damage the image of Prosecco.*

While the process of applying protected designation of origin to Prosecco is still in train and has yet to produce visible results, the producers of Valdobbiadene are very much aware of the need to develop a way of "Valdobbiadenizing" their wine, though it's proving as difficult to achieve as the name of the town is to pronounce.

Maria Luisa Dalla Costa* described the distinctive factors which mark the production of the *cru* Valdobbiadene-Conegliano DOCG Prosecco Superiore Rive:* "These quality wines are subject to severe restrictions. The vines have to be cultivated by hand and have a lower yield per hectare. It's enough to look at a photo of some of the *rive* to understand the extreme challenges the winegrowers face in working and maintaining the vines. It was this that prompted the legislative decision to introduce into the new regulations governing the DOCG the term *rive* followed by the specific name of the smallholding (*Rive di Santo Stefano, Rive di Vidor, Rive di Col San Martino,* etc.)* If you ask a viticulturist of Prosecco how old their vineyards are, they'll tell you ten, twenty, forty years old. But in the case of the *rive*, they'll tell you it varies a lot. This is because where vines are cultivated on *rive* it is extremely unwise to uproot an old vine completely to plant new stock, due to the way the soil is formed* and the incline of the *rive*, which can sometimes be between sixty and eighty degrees.

"As a result, it's more practical to cut back an old vine which is worn out or diseased to just above the surface of the soil and replace it with a new vine planted alongside. Doing it this way means that the roots of the old vine remain in the subsoil and keep the earth compacted, so there is no risk of dangerous landslides, while in the mean time the new vines start to spread.

"There is also very clear evidence for the fact that the vines planted on the *rive* have a much lower yield, because of the great differences in the ages of the vines and because they're less closely planted. On the other hand, however, in terms of quality, the organoleptic results are particularly rich and complex owing to the diversity of elements in the generational mix.

"Visitors who walk along the rows of vines on the *rive* can easily see the differences in the vine stocks. It's very common for example to see a row of young vines with thin stems sharing the row and alternating with old thick-stemmed vines, some of them ninety years old."

Epilogue

The unification of Italy was conditioned by the strategic designs of the powerful European nations, in disregard of any issues over their sense of identity which might arise among the new country's citizens. The aftermath of unification led to the exodus of over thirteen million Italians, approximately half the country's population in 1867. The migrants had to endure gruelling circumstances in countries that were initially unwelcoming, and took on servile jobs which the natives didn't want to do. They entered various kinds of employment and encouraged other Italians to make the move. In 1940 Italy entered the war, and the Italian migrants who were resident in the UK were abandoned to a tragic situation; the respective governments, in their race for power, were unconcerned with their fate. Once the war was over, there were agreements between European governments to supply labour shortages; Italians took on a range of hard, demanding jobs in coal mines and brick factories. But they were determined to improve their conditions of life and invented new activities for themselves; they spread consumer goods that were once the preserve of the well-off and made them available to the poorer classes. Keeping their ties to their homeland, they encouraged the export of products and ways of life from a country that hadn't been able to give them the opportunity of earning a living.*

Their success was also due to the sense of national solidarity and the network of reciprocal help that existed between families, neighbours and fellow countrymen. It was this solidarity that contributed to lifting the poorest Italians out of their marginalization and wretchedness.*

It was in this context that Italian food came to be known outside Italy; the fact it entered into people's daily lives was the result of a collective effort. In the same way, the success of Prosecco is the result of the entire Italian people working together. Creativity, passion and love were the weapons with which Italians conquered in the past; today Italy is called upon to maintain the bonds and the affection which unites its people.*

"Even I myself felt like a Prosecco soldier." (Ossie Gray)

Today the world is increasingly globalized, and the antagonism that was once seen among nations has now shifted to the multinational giants. The contemporary form of imperialism is seen in consumer goods: market share is fought over by the international companies in the name of material prosperity, the ultimate goal of human activity. The identities of populations are changing rapidly, as new social realities emerge. The great hotels, with all their luxuries, are the temples of the modern age, where businessmen meet each other. Unlike the old Christian cathedrals, the expressions of a past in which people believed they had to suffer in order to obtain divine grace, the grand hotels reflect a view of the world which aims at building paradise on earth. Soft armchairs and sofas replace pews, while the veneration formerly given to saints and martyrs is now bestowed on billionaire businessmen who move about the world on private jets, representing purely material values. New York shows the new priorities: small churches huddle here and there next to vast skyscrapers stretching up into the heavens. In modern Asian cities, there seem to be no buildings with a spiritual significance at all; if they do exist, you need to look hard for them.

Today groups of companies compete with each other in unpredictable ways. Emigrants in search of fortune, salespeople, restaurateurs – they're all like modern armies. In Alessandro Allegretti's words, the sales reps for food products felt like frontline soldiers; to all those who have contributed to the present-day success of Prosecco, a congratulatory glass should be raised. But few of them feel victorious: many feel, with a certain bitterness, that in the end the only winner is the product itself, which now follows its own path. In the hyperactive lives they led before, continually focused on projects to carry out and goals to achieve, they've lost the sense of time, which has sped by too fast. They remember the boredom they used to feel back home in the villages and towns they left in order to find a more active and fulfilling existence.

Back there, where time hung heavy, there was room for memories, moments of idleness in which to daydream and abandon yourself to feelings of self-satisfaction or self-pity. The always cheerful Gerardo Coppola says: "It's not nostalgia for the past – some of that you prefer to forget – but the sensation that something has gone missing in the new path you've taken." If soldiers in the past lost their lives in battle, now there are people who feel as if they live out their present battles pursuing phantoms.

"You live happily if you don't dwell on past successes and if you easily forget past failures." (Enzo Bucciol)

Thirty years after Prosecco was first introduced in the UK it's time to draw some conclusions. Not many of the people who played a leading role in its success are satisfied, and spend their days playing golf with friends. This is what Raffaele Addio has decided to do; he took early retirement while still young and still capable of making good profits. Roberto Gardetto is also an exception: he keeps himself happy by immersing himself in family life and in sporting activities. He goes running regularly in the Surrey pine woods with all the energy of a young boy: "If you stay still, it's like a vintage car getting rusty," he says, with a metaphor all his own. Andrea Riva continues to sit quietly in the corner of his restaurant, happy to talk to his customers about literature or yesterday's rugby match. Arnie Onisto cultivates the brightly coloured dahlias and hydrangeas in his garden and watches the seasons pass, something he never noticed when he worked at Florians. Ermanno Taverna is content with the companionship of his wife Anna, despite what his grandfather used to tell him: "When your wife turns sixty, replace her with two thirty-year-olds." Ermanno fishes for mackerel on the Brighton seafront. He's glad his son Alberto continues to manage Il Duomo and to have been able to give a house to each of his three grandchildren. Rinaldo Mollura likes the sea. He's planning to sell up everything in the next four years, since he no longer wants anything to do with business and money-making, to retire to an island eight thousand kilometres away – he's already identified which one. "My family and friends will come and visit me. We'll eat the fish I've caught. It'll be the best restaurant in the world. I'll be able to look at the sea, smell it and hear it as much as I like, until I start to get bored and time starts to hang heavy."

Few restaurateurs can find balance in their life, due to the demands of business and family. Some have failed in both of these spheres and have no plans for retirement, since they wouldn't know how to relax with their wives, with whom in any case they're often at odds. Other Italian restaurateurs living in the UK are worn out and even find it difficult to raise a natural smile. Their faces show the negative effects of the passage of time – a bit like old wine when it oxidizes and turns vinegary. You can't find happiness in the present moment, since you're always looking to the future to improve and innovate. "Life slips away,"

Peppino Battocchi used to complain, as he saw his days go by attending to his customers' demands. The need to find a different way of life, the reason so many discontented individuals migrate elsewhere, is never solved; an inner emptiness remains, which you try to fill with frenetic activity. Gian Piero Gorietti sums up our forebears' old adage: "You're happy if you're contented with what you've got."

But if those Italians who are getting on in years tend to become negative in outlook, the young – in years and in energy – look to the future with optimism. Enzo Cassini, who knows very well that what comes into fashion doesn't last long, is filled with renewed enthusiasm by the restaurant Assunta Madre, which has recently opened near New Bond Street. He thinks the Italians still have a lot to say. The brothers Donato and Paolo Cillo are busy promoting the products of their native Basilicata in Liverpool, and the Sardinian distributor Roberto Zintu and other Sardinian friends are doing the same for their island. Matteo Bonomelli from Verona goes round London restaurants presenting a new food product, *culatello stagionato* (dried salted pork) steeped in Amarone wine – which his father Vittorino, a butcher, makes. The Tuscan Nicola Dini, who came to London after graduating in philosophy and is now the manager of the Russian restaurant Mari Vanna, puts his philosophical training to good use in describing the complexity of everyday human relationships, while the very youthful sommelier Giacomo Morlacchi, who worked in Toto's, looks forward to future opportunities:

EPILOGUE

"I'm fluent in French and English, and now I'd like to go to Germany to learn German."

It is the younger generation that is most exposed to the uses and abuses of information technology. This can encourage a physical passivity in contrast to the dynamic outlook of the young Italians just described. The pleasure of outdoor games has been replaced by virtual gaming on a computer screen. Sales, love affairs, friendships are all mediated by modern gadgets. Technology has modified the ways we socialize and extinguished the desire to make experiences our own by reflecting on them and absorbing them. Giorgio Casadei, now retired but in his day an outstanding sales rep with a remarkable ability to communicate, wonders if salesmen still need the human contact of going round from door to door to achieve results. "Absolutely," says Marco Cremonese in Aberdeen. "Modern society is sick and in need of psychological help. For me every sale is a real pleasure."

Alessandro Marchesan recalls, with an air of melancholy, how "Prosecco cheered me up whenever I felt down – it brought a childlike happiness back". Many Italian emigrants working abroad hear the call of their homeland – like Paolo Della Puppa in New York, who dreams of the old pergola back in Italy, where he'd eat a piece of Asiago cheese and some salad picked from his parents' garden – tasting better than anything he'd eaten since. For Italians far from their country, Italian food brings back memories of their youth. Memories of a happy childhood make us wish for a more people-friendly world.

Hopefully this story will encourage those who are dissatisfied with their lives to find another path: the world is full of opportunities for the young and the not so young, for the experienced and the less experienced. Carlo Distefano proves it: he had zero experience of the sector when he started out, and he now controls a business empire.

The aim of this book has been to bring together many personal accounts of running Italian restaurants in the UK and promoting Prosecco. I've preferred to let my witnesses speak for themselves. Lorenzo Castiglioni praised the spontaneity of emigrants: "Leaving their own country behind allowed many of them to find themselves." My lack of diplomacy may upset some, including my British readers; the British like to be ironic and self-deprecating, but they're not so fond of irony when they are the butt of a foreigner's joke. To avoid any possible misunderstanding, I take this opportunity to renew Enzo Di Nolfi's call to offer up sincere thanks to the British, who have been so welcoming to the Italians for so many years.

As I was telling my story, I've sometimes felt that I should give it a little more reflection, but, if I'd stopped too much to think how to say things better, I wouldn't have got further than the title. As Domenico Taravella says: "If you think too much, you'll never create anything." My intention was to tell the story of Prosecco's success through the significant experiences of the people who were involved in that success. Yet I've found myself describing other aspects of their lives, both serious and comic (and often it's hard to distinguish the two). This is the involuntary outcome of writing inspired by memory, which tries to give meaning and character to seemingly insignificant situations, which nevertheless bring a smile to one's face and show us the positive side of things. "I often think about the old days, and they always make me laugh" – so says Toni Rovai as he tells one of his amusing anecdotes. This is a small truth we can all acknowledge. Francesco Maschio adds another important consideration, speaking of his friend Antonio Melina: "Everyone who comes into contact with him likes him." I hope this story will be read at least by those who have really lived it, so they recognize themselves in its pages. But perhaps that's unlikely. Teo Catino says he has read only a couple of books in his life. "Who wants to spend their time reading?" For Teo life itself is exciting; you don't need to waste time on books.

There are excellent Italian wines, but only a few have conquered a global market. Some producers of Prosecco from Valdobbiadene and Conegliano or the Asolo and Montello hillsides are convinced that the wine's success is entirely down to its quality. The story I've told here attributes part of that success to the people who were involved in it. If in the process the world of winemaking has lost something of its poetic aura – so important in marketing wine – that's because my focus has been on the people who are the real creators of that world: wine as a human product.

Notes

p. 5, Basically, Italians have introduced food products into those foreign countries where there was already an Italian presence. The sommelier Dino Bisaccia, originally from the province of Matera, referring to his experience at the Savoy Hotel, observed the difference between the French and the Italians in their manner of serving wines: "The Frenchman offers the bottle to the customer with both hands, showing the label and waiting for approval. The Italian puts the bottle between his legs, highlighting the effort of uncorking it with a beautiful smile."

PART I

p. 13, Italians of various kinds – monks, bankers, musicians, architects and artists – have been coming to Britain for centuries, though this never became a mass phenomenon.

p. 14, McKee, Francis, *Ice Cream and Immorality*, in *Oxford Symposium on Food and Cookery 1991. Public Eating. Proceedings*, ed. Harlan Walker (London: Prospect Books, 1991), p. 191.

p. 17, Sources vary as to the exact number of Italians lost in the tragedy, but it is believed to be between 446 and 486.

p. 17, Contini, Mary, *Dear Olivia: An Italian Journey of Love and Courage* (Edinburgh: Canongate Books, 2006).

p. 18, The retailer Antonio Bavaro, whose parents Giuseppe and Carolina arrived in Bedford in the 1940s, says that the first Italians who bought houses there replaced the typical British flower garden with a vegetable plot, in which they cultivated the vegetables they'd grown at home. Today producers of Italian origin are an important part of British rural life.

p. 22, Charles, Baron Forte, originally Carmine Forte, and born in a village in the province of Frosinone in 1908, came to the UK in 1911 with his parents. Starting from nothing, he succeeded in building an empire comprising 800 hotels and more than 1,000 restaurants. The company employed about 70,000 people. Lord Forte remained head of the group until the age of eighty, when he left the directorship to his son Rocco Forte. He passed away in 2007 at the age of ninety-eight.

p. 22, At the time, Franco Santoro was a sales representative working for the importers Hedges & Butler, before subsequently establishing his own importing firm, Sunshine Wine. In the 1990s, together with his children, he set up the company Vinissimo, which is still in business. Franco passed away in 2011. Paolo and his sister Chantal continue their father's work.

p. 23, Gerardo is joint owner, with the Iranian Amir Rezaei, of Q Verde in Kew.

p. 24, In 1993 Emanuele and Pamela Orto opened Il Piccolo at Prudhoe, in Northumberland. Today they run Il Piccolo in Corbridge. Pamela McNulty met Emanuele during a skiing holiday in the Val Di Susa in Piedmont, where the Sicilian Emanuele was working as a chef. They fell in love, and she moved to Italy to work with him. Then they settled in England, where they became popular promoters of new Italian foods.

p. 24, Their sons are Steve, Mark and Jonathan. In 2013 they created a Prosecco bar outside the restaurant, inspired by the bars of Venice.

p. 26, In Italy the cuisine of upper-middle-class families was characterized by formality of service and presentation.

p. 27, Leonardo Barolo, for example, a promoter of Italian fashion, actively incited violence as part of the student movement while studying in Padua during the 1970s. He moved to England for political reasons.

p. 28, Roberto Simeone is a Member of the Institute of Hospitality (MIH) and of AIBES, the Italian Association of Barmen and Business Supporters.

p. 28, There are some exceptions: Cornwall, for example, a county of about half a million inhabitants, and not fully integrated into England. The restaurateur Camillo Baggio, who ran restaurants in Redruth, said years ago: "Cornwall is a very beautiful part of the country, but it is not a land of smiles. The inhabitants are closed and mistrustful. It will be difficult to make Prosecco popular here." Based on recent personal experience, the author takes a much more positive view of Cornwall as an attractive county which offers good food and whose people are very open-minded.

p. 31, Claudio Compri and his wife Patrizia run Enocibus in the historic centre of Verona.

p. 35, Valvona & Crolla is a deli-restaurant in Edinburgh selling Italian foods and wines. The name refers to the partnership in 1934 of two Italian families, the Valvonas and the Crollas, who had previously run separate shops. The Crollas came from Fontitune in the Picinisco district of the province of Frosinone. Today the deli and restaurant are run by Philip and Mary Contini, descendants of one of the founding families. Donatantonio was a shop located on Clerkenwell Road in Holborn. It was opened in 1902 by Luigi Doñatantonio, who came from Minori on the Amalfi Coast. Today Donatantonio is a supplier

of food products. The Terroni delicatessen, which later
became Terroni & Sons, dates back to 1878, when it was
founded by Luigi Terroni, also on Clerkenwell Road. It
is still in business today, run by Antonio Alfano.

p. 38, The Tiggis in the Trafford Centre was a very big
restaurant. It boasts a record of serving over 1,700 customers in a single day. On one occasion, soon after it had
opened, the head chef was seized with panic. In the middle
of a service he left the restaurant and came back dressed
as a *carabiniere*. He took up a position in the middle of
the large dining hall and directed people as though they
were at a rally in the town square. Today there are three
restaurants occupying the space of the former Tiggis.

p. 39, Nicola La Verghetta came to London in the 1970s
from Vasto in the Abruzzo. After eighteen months' naval
service in various parts of Italy, he realized that Vasto was
not a town in which he wanted to spend his whole life.
He took the first opportunity to leave, and so began his
adventure in England. He was associated with many restaurants, as manager, business partner and finally owner.
Nicola's life is rich in experiences of all kinds, lived with
generosity and passion. He has always found time for
everything: for his girlfriend, his ex-wife, his lovers, his
daughter Paola and his friends, for football, travel and the
promotion of Prosecco.

p. 39, These are the restaurants set up by Otello and Elio
Scipioni in London: Trattoria Otello, Trattoria Toscana,
Il Porcellino, La Dolce Vita, Il Girasole, Villa dei Cesari.

p. 40, Parmigiano Reggiano, Prosecco and other products
have benefited from the support of restaurant waiters.
The popularity of Parmesan in the UK and elsewhere in
the world is due to Italian waiters' habit of appearing at

the table after serving the pasta dishes with the cheese and a grater and asking: "Would you like some Parmesan?" Italians also appear with a long wooden pepper mill for dusting this spicy aphrodisiac over every plate. According to Enrico Toscani, the pepper mill was a symbol of virility, matching the image the Italians wanted to display.

p. 41, Ermanno Taverna lost his father Carlo when he was sixteen. "Since I had two younger brothers, I looked for work and went to see the parish priest at Fornovo di Taro in Emilia, because back then priests had an influence over employers. The priest said to me, "Your father was one of those socialist scum. As long as I'm the priest of this parish, you'll never get a decent job." Humiliated, I went back to my mother Aldina, who wept for a couple of days. I left for France, where I worked at the Georges V Hotel in Paris, then I moved to Geneva, Lausanne, Zurich, St Moritz and to Montreal. I came back to Europe (Hamburg), and in 1965 I arrived in London and worked as front of house manager at the Savoy Hotel, for Mario and Franco and the Grand Metropolitan Group. Finally I opened my own restaurants." Ermanno speaks four languages fluently, and failing to get the priest's recommendation turned out to be the making of him, but the man's words still rankle.

p. 42, Mr Chow in Knightsbridge was opened by Michael Chow in 1968. The menu was Chinese, but the food had to be served by Italians. Nicola La Verghetta spent eight years at Mr Chow and says of the owner: "Michael's parents were famous figures in the Chinese theatre. They sent the young Michael to London to study. During the Maoist revolution, his parents were interned for political reasons, and Michael stayed in England and took the opportunity to travel. After gaining a lot of experience, he opened a chain of restaurants located in various cities around the world. A charismatic personality, he inspired many Italians who worked for him in Knightsbridge." Many of Mr Chow's former waiters and managers set up new restaurants of their own. These include Roberto Mangoni, Augusto Tramontano, Antonio Trapani, Sandro Tobi, Mario Pagetti, Fabio Terrinoni, Nicola La Verghetta, Juan Rio, Alfonso Cretella, Mario Basilico, Giancarlo Saba and others.

p. 42, The salesman Giorgio Casadei, of Enotria Winecellars, concentrated in the 1990s on Chinese restaurants and succeeded in supplying wine to 180 of them. Almost all added Prosecco to their wine lists. Giorgio reveals the secret of his success: "You just have to tell the Chinese what to do, because they still don't know about wine."

p. 43, Cipriani, Arrigo, *Harry's Bar, a Venetian Legend* (Venezia: Alcione Editore, 2010), p. 26.

p. 43, The story of Mario Cassandro and Franco Lagattolla, owners of La Terrazza, Tiberio and other restaurants, is told in Alasdair Scott Sutherland's book *The Spaghetti Tree: Mario and Franco and the Trattoria Revolution* (London: Primavera Books, 2009). This is a detailed study of certain aspects of the Italian restaurant trade from the 1960s onwards, crediting the dissemination of the first real Italian cuisine in the UK to these two restaurateurs.

p. 43, Walter Mariti, now retired, was a successful restaurateur. He opened Pontevecchio, Factotum, La Meridiana and Pontenuovo in Chelsea (now called Riccardo's, run by his son Riccardo).

p. 44, The "New Wave Italian" included the River Café, Gino Taddei's Cibo and L'Altro, Andrea Riva's Riva restaurant and Franco Papa and Arnoldo Onisto's Florians.

Other restaurants which introduced a more authentically Italian style of cuisine were Stefano Tiraboschi's Caruso, Adolfo Tiraboschi's La Buca, Giuseppe and Pamela Turi's Enoteca Turi, Adolfo Tiraboschi and Alex Palano's Basilico, Casale Franco in Islington, belonging to Franco Pensa and his brothers, Ciro Corsaro's Made in Italy and Mauro Sanna's Olivo, all the way to Andrea Ippolito's Pizza Metro Pizza, culminating in the A–Z group's Zafferano in 1995.

p. 46, Leonardo Di Canto, originally from Trentinara, a village near Paestum in the Salerno area, owns a wholesale distribution company for wine and food. He lives in Scotland with his Scottish wife Sharon.

p. 47, Mario Molino came to London from Naples in 1958 to study. He was from Spaccanapoli, the road that runs through the historical centre of the city. In 1963 he worked as a dishwasher at Il Pirata in Sutton, a restaurant owned by Ermanno Bozzoni and Silvano Sacchi, proprietors of the L'Alpino chain. In 1966 he became the pizza chef at the first Pizza Express. More recently, he ran Da Mario on Gloucester Road in London, until his death in 2011. He wrote an autobiography, as yet unpublished. He left the management of the restaurant to his son Marco.

p. 49, "*Figa*" is slang for the female genitalia; "*bordello*" means "brothel".

p. 49, Cipriani, Arrigo, *Prigioniero di una stanza a Venezia* (*Prisoner in a Room in Venice*) (Milan: Feltrinelli, 2009), p. 49.

p. 49, The only Italian restaurants in Britain to have been awarded a Michelin star in recent years are the River Café and Locanda Locatelli.

p. 50, Quoted by Domenico Buffarini in *Il popolo degli uomini* (*The People of Men*) (Vicenza: Editore Clan Nazionale Seniores Scouts Italiani, CNGEI, 1992), p. 54.

p. 51, Perhaps it's time to set up a system of drug testing for chefs too, as for professional cyclists?

p. 57, William Hill, Coral and Ladbrokes are the most widespread betting chains. Coral and Ladbrokes merged recently. In the past the number of betting shops reached 15,000. Today, with the spread of betting on the Internet, the number has reduced and betting shops are most widespread in poor areas.

p. 59, Wilkins, W.H., 'The Italian Aspect', in *The Destitute Alien in Great Britain*, ed. Arnold Henry White (London: W. Swan Sonnenschein & Co., 1892), p. 152.

p. 62, "My friend Umberto Scomparin, a true son of the Veneto, brought the regional tradition of drinking an *ombra* [lit. "shadow", but meaning "a small glass of wine", see second note to p. 88] to the restaurants he worked in, offering a glass of Prosecco before the meal and one afterwards. I used to watch him as he performed this ritual. He was a great ambassador for Prosecco." (Enzo Cassini)

p. 64, In 2018 the import duty on a single 75cl bottle of Prosecco Spumante is £2.77, to which must be added 20% VAT.

p. 67, Cipriani, Arrigo, *Prigioniero di una stanza a Venezia*, p. 41.

p. 68, Le Piat d'Or was a French wine, unknown in France, produced specifically for the British market. It was once one of the best-selling French wines in the UK.

p. 70, Nicola Lovato, marketing representative for Santa Margherita in the UK, is more specific: "Santa Margherita were the first to create Pinot Grigio, in 1961, making wine from the white grapes, responding to the need to invent a balanced wine for international markets."

p. 70, The wine merchant Alivini has been a substantial player in the market for food and wine over the past forty years. Gianni Segatta says that "Alivini was set up in 1975 with the aim of advancing and revolutionizing the perception of Italian food and wine, because importers at that time confined themselves to supplying known Italian products, and simply competed against each other over price. The company was founded by the Vignali brothers, Mauro and Giovanni, and Antonio Pirozzi. Over the years there have been changes to the company, which have included collaborations with individual traders such as Renato Trestini and with the Villa Banfi company."

PART II

p. 76, Trevisan restaurateurs were among the first in Italy to set up an active association (Cocofungo) which organized frequent cooking demonstrations based on seasonal ingredients: mushrooms, radicchio, etc.

p. 76, Giuseppe Mazzotti and Giuseppe Maffioli, who were both writers, journalists and gastronomes, promoted Trevisan culture in Italy.

p. 76, Some people stored the plants in a dung heap.

p. 77, Vianello, Angelo and Carpenè, Antonio, *La vite e il vino nella provincia di Treviso*, (*Vine and Wine in the Province of Treviso*) (Conegliano: Dario De Bastiani Editore, 1873), p. 3.

p. 78, Work in the vineyards – pruning the vines, harvesting, applying copper sulphate – was by no means the pleasant idyll it is sometimes depicted as. We are entitled to doubt the authenticity of that "passion for the land" which many wine producers go on about, while the actual work on the land is done by other people.

p. 80, Alessandro Marchesan was the wine buyer for a prestigious group that comprises restaurants in various cities around the world. In London this includes Zuma, Coya, The Arts Club, Oblix, Peyote, La Petite Maison and four branches of Roka. Alessandro is originally from Bessega, a small town near Bassano del Grappa, well known for its trade in plants.

p. 82, Dorino Sartor worked with the El Toulà group between 1964 and 1983. He then opened the trattoria Tony del Spin, located in the centre of Treviso.

p. 82, The founder of the El Toulà group (*"el toulà"* is "the barn" in Cortina) was Alfredo Beltrame – a charismatic restaurateur with a strong bond to Treviso. Alfredo opened his first restaurant in Jesolo in 1959. In 1961, his clientele sponsored the opening of Da Alfredo in Treviso. The same customers who frequented the tourist town of Cortina gave him financial support for the creation of El Toulà in Cortina in 1964, and later for restaurants in Rome, Ponzano, Paris, Tokyo, etc.

p. 84, Data at the end of 2017: the vineyards of Glera (the Prosecco grape) cover a total area of about 34,182 hectares. Around 29,654 hectares have traditionally been cultivated in the Veneto region, 4,528 hectares in the Friuli region. The area delimited by the Prosecco DOCG (8,088 hectares) is situated in the historic hilly region extending between Valdobbiadene and Conegliano, comprising fifteen districts. 1,644 hectares of Glera are cultivated on the hills of Asolo and Montello, with the appellation Asolo

Prosecco Superiore DOCG. The other appellations excluded from the DOCG area are Prosecco DOC Treviso, Prosecco DOC Trieste and Prosecco DOC, i.e. with no indication of region, covering the provinces of Udine (UD), Gorizia (GO), Pordenone (PN), Venice (VE), Padua (PD), Vicenza (VI) and Belluno (BL). Production is increasing. In addition to the Glera base varietal, the regulator allows for a maximum possible use of 15% from other varieties. Pinot and Chardonnay grapes are permitted. Glera is the native variety that guarantees the structural base of the Valdobbiadene-Conegliano appellation. Other native varietals such as Verdiso, Perera and Bianchetta contribute to the characteristic palate of Prosecco. These lesser varietals can also be used in quantities up to 15%. The Verdiso grape increases acidity and flavour. The Perera grape brings an aromatic bouquet. The Bianchetta grape makes Prosecco smoother in cold years, because it ripens earlier. It is cultivated in the highest, often almost inaccessible areas, and for this reason is heading for extinction. The most common types of Prosecco Spumante are Brut, the driest (the residual sugar may not exceed 12 g/l); Extra Dry (residual sugar around 16–17 g/l); and Dry (with the highest level of residual sugar, between 20 and 24 g/l).

p. 84, Dino Maule, son of viticulturists from Gambellara, spent the first and most important years of his career working for the Zonin family. He still considers the chairman of the firm, Gianni Zonin, his maestro. He subsequently took on the commercial management of several winemaking companies, including Mionetto of Valdobbiadene, where he met the author and collaborated with him. He still works in the trade at Valdobbiadene.

p. 86, The champenoise method requires a second fermentation and the trapping of foam in the bottle (to produce the bubbles). This takes longer and is more demanding than the Charmat-Martinotti system used for Prosecco, in which the process of trapping foam takes place in large steel containers. The technological evolution of the process of making sparkling wine (*"spumantizzazione"*) developed in the Valdobbiadene-Conegliano district plays a fundamental role in the quality of Prosecco as it's produced today.

p. 86, The Prosecco DOCG and DOC estates, covering 34,182 hectares, are divided up among a great number of producers owning an average of just over two hectares each. The actual scale of champagne production is pretty much the same.

p. 88, Ciborio was bought at the end of the 1950s by the seven Alfano brothers from Acquaviva Platani, in the Sicilian province of Caltanissetta. Ciborio specialized in the distribution of Italian foods and wines and made a major contribution to the introduction of new products across Great Britain. The eldest Alfano brother was called Salvatore, also known as Scheriffo: then came Carmelo, Pino, Carlo, Paolo, Vincenzo and Giovanni. The Alfanos closed down the business in 2007.

p. 88, The terms *ombra* (lit. "shade") and *ombretta* are used in the Veneto to indicate a small glass of wine. Among the speculations on the origin of the name, one goes back to the period of the Venetian Republic, when the stallholders selling wine in St Mark's Square took refuge from the hot sun in the shade of the Campanile.

p. 88, Sandro Bottega lost his father Aldo when he was young, and with the help of his mother Rosina, his brother Stefano and his sister Barbara, he immediately took over responsibility for salvaging the small distillery he had inherited. He started travelling around the world presenting grappa in blown-glass bottles. In 1993–94, in collaboration with local partners, he opened a shop in Taipei, one in Hong Kong and one in Singapore, devoted exclusively to the sale of grappa. White-gloved Chinese waiters poured from delicate glass bottles – grappa had arrived in the East. Today Bottega is also a popular Prosecco brand.

p. 89, Among the influential members of Winecellars were two "Masters of Wine": David Gleeve and Nicolas Belfrage.

p. 89, Among the sommeliers active in London during the late 1990s were Livio Italiani at the Conran Group's Sartoria; Antonio Cerilli, Luciana Girotto and Bruno Besa of the Stefano Cavallini restaurant in the Halkin Hotel; Luigi Lago of Toto's; and Dino Bisaccia at Caravaggio. Since 2007, the Italian Sommelier Association (AIS) of the UK has become a very dynamic organization under the directorship of Andrea Rinaldi.

p. 90, Rorato, Giampiero, *Il Prosecco di Conegliano-Valdobbiadene* (Nonta, Udine: Morganti Editori, 2006), p. 11.

p. 92, Some of Fabbris's acquaintances who promoted Prosecco were: Giuliano Ferrari (Villa Bianca), Antonio Trapani (Montpeliano and Toto's), Iginio Santin (Santini and L'Incontro), Walter Mariti (Pontevecchio and Pontenuovo), Enzo Bucciol (Balzac Bistro), Pietro Rosignoli (Poissonerie de l'Avenue) and Lillo Militello (Concordia Notte).

p. 92, Lunardi's clients included Mario & Sandro in Barnet, Franco's in East Barnet, Trevi in Finchley, Enzo's in Enfield and La Campagnola in Victoria.

p. 92, Those who were involved with Ciao Italia and regular purchased Prosecco included Gabriele Di Michele's Il

Giardino in Cobham; Franco Langella's Spaghetti Junction in Teddington; Ermanno Taverna's Trattoo in Kensington and La Terrazza Est in the City of London; Gianfranco Carraro's restaurant Carraro in Battersea; Mario Arricale's The Orchard in Hampstead; Carlo Barbieri's Villa dei Fiori in Golders Green; Attilio Cepollina and Emanuele Maffi's Terrazza in Ashford. Today the names of these restaurants have changed, and they have different owners. The dynamics of the restaurant trade in the UK are different from those in Italy, where trattorie and restaurants are handed down from father to son.

p. 93, After this, another sale was clinched with the wine merchants Majestic by two young men, Paolo Nolasco and Angelo Cane, who subsequently set up Vinum, a firm of importers that is still in business. Majestic did not go on to place another order.

p. 93, At the end of the 1980s, the winemakers producing Prosecco adopted the champagne-style bottle as well as the mushroom-shaped cork, and tried to embellish the appearance of the bottle with gleaming gold and silver labels.

p. 93, The bottle with the loop of string had a drawback: the champagne cork was fully inserted into the neck of the bottle and proved difficult to pull out. Sometimes the neck broke, and waiters would cut their hands. To overcome this problem the company provided corkscrews shaped like a gun.

p. 94, In the summer of 1991, in the L'Altro restaurant in Portobello, during a Channel Four interview with a famous actress, Gino Taddei offered glasses of Prosecco to the production team. The director filmed the Prosecco as it was decanted into the carafe and inserted the episode into the programme, thus giving the wine considerable publicity.

p. 95, There were four Italians in the Enotria team: Giorgio Casadei, Remo Casadei, Giuseppe Tomaselli, Vincenzo Falanga; and a French manager, Eric Bernau. In the North-West, Nick McNelly started the introduction of Prosecco in Manchester and Preston. John Hillis looked after Scotland; Chris Malchin handled the more prestigious clients; and Simon Stagnell the food shops.

p. 95, Among Enotria's clients was Spaghetti House, founded by Simone Lavarini and Lorenzo Fraquelli in 1955. Other restaurants included Mario Pagetti's Signor Sassi and Scalini; Sandro Tobi's Sale e Pepe, Sambuca and Sandrini in Knightsbridge; Luciano Beccarelli and Sergio Dellanzo's Val Taro, near Leicester Square; the Chinese restaurant Lee Hoo Fook in Soho; the Thai restaurant Bangkok in South Kensington; and Bibendum in Chelsea. Among the specialist wine merchants were Corney & Barrow in Portobello and Jerry's Wines and Spirits in Soho. There was an Italian presence in all these areas, and as a result these shops sold more Prosecco than others.

p. 95, The collaboration with F&S lasted three years. Then there was a pause, during which Mionetto slackened their aggressive strategy. F&S, the official supplier for De Cecco pasta, had been set up by Domenico Farace, known as Mimì, in 1981. The firm was managed by his son, Pantaleone, known as Leo. Shortly after Mimì died, F&S was sold to another food supplier, Donatantonio. During their collaboration, Mionetto's sales fell, and there was a decrease in the number of new Prosecco clients. F&S was active in developing sales of Prosecco in small food shops – including Camisa & Son, a deli which opened in 1961 in the heart of Soho; Lina De Angelis's La Picena in

Knightsbridge; Marcello Bizio and Salvatore Maggiulli's Salumeria Napoli on Northcote Road; Gazzano's on Farringdon Road, a shop going back for generations, and formerly run by Joe Gazzano; and Ferrari's Gastronomia in Islington. Other F&S activities were the development of the Scottish market via the supplier Quattro Stagioni, run by Tony Turner, and the introduction of Prosecco in the Newcastle area via Bruno Tavasso's Euromarket. Two F&S salesmen, Franco De Mennato and Francesco Rocca, would later found their own companies, two food distribution businesses, while continuing to promote Prosecco in their catalogues. In the same period, Mionetto collaborated with Bruno Bettini and his son Andrew. In the 1970s, Bruno Bettini worked for the supplier Hedges & Butler, one of the first importers of Italian wines. Like many restaurateurs, Bruno had a passion for card games. His best clients were his card-playing companions. Through Bettini, Prosecco was introduced to Roberto Ballerini's Capanna in Cobham, Toni di Michele's Vecchia Roma in Hampton Court and Chapter One in Locksbottom, belonging to Giovanni Ulivi and his partners.

p. 98, The first client in Edinburgh to promote Prosecco was the food shop Valvona & Crolla Ltd. In Glasgow, the brothers Piero and Sandro Sarti had a very high opinion of Prosecco. Their restaurant and shop Fratelli Sarti, in Bath Street, played an active role in the promotion of Prosecco and was its leading purchaser in the whole of Scotland. In 1998, inspired by Mionetto's ideas, the brothers opened Proseccheria Sarti in Glasgow.

p. 98, For over ten years, Massimiliano Jacobacci has managed his company FortyFive10 Ltd, specializing in distribution on behalf of prestigious Italian wine estates.

p. 98, Gregorio Stabile's clients were Chinawhite, on Air Street, near Piccadilly Circus; Cantina Italia in Islington, belonging to the Sardinian brothers Pier Gianni and Sebastiano Meloni; Spago in South Kensington, owned by Angelo Felici and Michele Pastore, known as Lillo; Franco D'Alessio's L'Antico on the King's Road; Pino Alfano's Galiano's. Outside London, his clients were Pasquale Sarpi's Villa Rosa in Egham; Diego Burzotta's La Carbonara in Chobham; Francesco Beni's pizzeria chain Don Beni, operating in the Windsor area; and Nicola De Paola's Da Vinci restaurant in Poole.

p. 100, Alessandro Maschio, producer of grappa and Prosecco, has no doubt about this. With two uncles – regular grappa-drinkers – aged over a hundred and two more approaching that age, Alessandro is convinced that wine and grappa prolong life.

p. 101, The Italian Continental Store distributor in Maidenhead was among the first to promote Prosecco in Berkshire. The company was and is run by Rosario Sardo, who is of Sicilian origin. His family came from Acquaviva Platani, in the province of Caltanissetta. Salvatore, Rosario's uncle, came to England at the age of eighteen to pick cucumbers in the fields near Slough. He brought over his parents and his brothers, and with them started up a food shop in Slough in May 1968. Carmelo, Salvatore's brother and Rosario's father, worked nearby as a lorry driver in the High Wycombe area, where many Italians lived. In the evening after work, Carmelo loaded the van with characteristic Sicilian products, including provolone cheese, and sold them to Italian working people. His grandfather died while still young and left the management of the shop to his three sons Carmelo,

Salvatore and Calogero, known as Lillo. Salvatore later opened an Italian shop in Chertsey, while Lillo moved to Italy. In 1990 Rosario went into partnership with his father and developed the distributor Italian Continental Store.

Other distributors of Prosecco were G&R, owned by Rocco Tanzarella from Ostuni in Puglia, a creative individual who later started producing Altamura bread; Alfonso Amitrano's Sorrento Express; Luigi Fulmine and Raffaele Addio's Mondo Food; Annessa Imports, belonging to the siblings John, Domenico and Giovanna Annessa; Franco, Chantal and Paolo Santoro's Vinissimo; and Fiandaca, owned by Alfie Fiandaca and his son Andrea. The supplier Lea & Sandeman brought Prosecco into independent shops and into their own distribution network. Andrew Pavli added it to his Wimbledon Wine Cellars.

p. 102, Giovanni Mionetto passed away on 8th March 2014.

p. 103, For years Prosecco in Great Britain had been identified with Mionetto, the only firm that was seeking out unusual and effective ways to distribute their products. The Mionetto family brought to the promotion of Prosecco their devotion to the land – not only because of the fecundity of its vineyards, but because of its artistic links to cities like Venice and Treviso. Producers of Prosecco and of other Italian wines travelled the world promoting their own wines before and after Mionetto. But no Italian winemaking company staked such significant investment on the construction of their own sales organizations, up until the late 1980s and early 1990s, with their own offices and staff, in countries such as Germany, the UK, Japan and the USA. The other winemakers confined foreign travel to their owners; few allowed themselves an export manager who would attend wine fairs and seek out local distributors.

p. 103, An observation made by Gianni Veronese, a former rep at Mionetto.

p. 103, Stefano Cadamuro, manager for private clients' accounts, worked at Mionetto for thirty years.

p. 103, Valdobbiadene never acknowledged the Mionetto family's contribution to its prestige. Other producers worked hard to take advantage of what they had initiated.

p. 103, "*Se ze par queo, par adesso, el ceuo i meo ga za fato!*"

p. 103, Today Attilio Mionetto is promoting – in partnership with Stefano Cadamuro – Colderove, his own brand of Prosecco.

p. 106, For reasons associated with the payment of tax on wine, the figure of the sales representative working to a commission, popular in Italy, is almost unknown in the UK. The salesmen who work for distributors are employees remunerated with salaries and bonuses. Marco Cremonese, from Naples, is one of the few freelance salesmen with experience in Italy. He worked with his father Vittorio in Campania for a well-known spumante producer. When he arrived in Scotland in 2000, he set himself up in the area between Glasgow, Edinburgh and Aberdeen, acting as an agent on behalf of various wine producers. Salesmen with experience in Italy usually achieve good results in the UK. Francesco Boscherino has experienced both markets and states his preference for working in Britain.

p. 109, In cosmopolitan London, potential clients come in all ages and types. Older purchasers will be at ease with salesmen of their own age; younger clients will prefer to deal with someone like themselves. Shared interests bring people together and bring about mutual understanding, which makes a commercial relationship easier to develop. In

NOTES

the British wine market, suppliers will look for sales staff of various nationalities: Turks for Turkish restaurants, Chinese for the Chinese, etc. Salesmen also specialize according to the potential clients they must approach, who may work in fashion, hospitals, hairdressing and universities.

p. 115, Dalbir is proud to have brought producers of Prosecco di Valdobbiadene such as Col Vetoraz and De Faveri into the British market.

p. 117, Bruno Zoccola, owner of the Valentina chain of delis, was the first to appreciate Roger's qualities as a salesman.

PART III

p. 122, The restaurants started by Alvaro Maccioni were Alvaro, Aretusa, Alvaro Pizza e Pasta, La Famiglia and La Nassa. Alvaro passed away in November 2013, at the age of seventy-six. La Famiglia is still in business, run by his daughter Marietta and his son-in-law Fabio Cozari. The style of cooking is still Alvaro's.

p. 122, Il Cappuccetto was sold in 2012, after fifty years under the same owner.

p. 123, Piero Quaradeghini was the first restaurateur to purchase an entire pallet of Prosecco directly from Italy. Over the next ten years, the two brothers acquired new restaurants in various areas of London. For a time the group employed the chef Alberico Penati as a consultant.

p. 123, The following all worked at Pizza Pucci: the brothers Luigi and Giorgio Colazzo, Angelo Camassa, Maurizio Selci, Franco Pensa, Sergio Vantaggiato, Carlo Cataldi. In the Seventies, according to Luigi Colazzo, the general manager of La Pappardella, the Pucci pizzerias and La Bersagliera functioned as a kind of school for modern

229

pizza chefs and introduced the pizza cooked directly in the oven: "Their pizzas came closer to the popular Italian version than the kind then being offered in Britain, which were cooked in a pan."

Other early clients included Rinaldo Pierini's La Genova in the heart of Mayfair (Pierini, originally from Genoa, claims to have been the first to introduce *pesto genovese*); Giovanni Guglielmoni's L'Abetone in Winchmore Hill, North London; Mamma Mia in Sheen, belonging to the Giannini siblings Leonardo, Giuseppe and Rosa; and Giulio Comoli's La Verbanella in Knightsbridge.

The first regular Prosecco clients outside London were Villa Bianca in Frimley, Villa Romana in Camberley, Il Borgo in Egham and Number Ten in Virginia Water. Ownership of these restaurants alternated between Rino Testa, Raffaele Gambardella, Paolo Fattore and Roberto Mangoni. These and others, such as Roberto Castagna and Pasquale Sarpi, were the driving forces behind Italian cuisine in Surrey. In the Manchester area, the supplier Tirreno Wine and Food, owned by the Sicilian Carlo Capaldi, was responsible for the introduction of Prosecco. Among his clients in the Manchester area were Domenico Pettinicchio's Portobello and Marcello Giannini's Marcello's. Cocotoo in Manchester deserves a special mention. The proprietors were Alfiero Centamore from Rome and Carlo Distefano. This restaurant occupied a railway arch, and Alfiero had a copy of the frescoes in the Sistine Chapel painted on its vault. The job kept a talented artist busy for more than a year. When the restaurant was sold, the new Indian owner immediately got rid of that expensive work of art. In Formby, near Liverpool, Gabriele Gervasoni from Val d'Aosta introduced local residents to Italian food in his restaurant Don Luigi.

Marcello Bizio was a disinterested promoter of Prosecco from the late 1980s onwards, when he sold his café, Drury. From Lecce in Puglia, he knew Prosecco because it was popular in his home town. He introduced it at Elio in Sanderstead, at Tony's Brasserie in Streatham and in numerous delicatessens. A passionate marathon runner, Marcello brought the same physical endurance to his work. Today, with his wife Marlena, he runs the food supplier Speciality Food, a specialist in cakes and sweets. Prosecco remains the only wine among the products in his catalogue.

p. 124, Among Prosecco's clients from the Veneto, Gianni Brunetta bought it regularly for his restaurant Il Salotto in Ealing. Lorenzo Castiglioni from Padua, manager of the Berni Inn in Guildford, took a risk by introducing it into his restaurant, which served traditional British cooking. The Berni company was originally founded by the brothers Franco and Aldo Berni from Bardi in Emilia-Romagna, who arrived in Wales in the first wave of emigrants from the town.

Ziani Restaurant in London, run by the Venetian Roberto Colusso, was among its first purchasers, as was Alberto Favalessa, who ran L'Antico in Henley-on-Thames. Sergio Perin, from Corbanese, promoted Prosecco to Ruskins, in the City of London. More recent and younger arrivals include Simon Piovesan, originally from Asolo, owner of the Due Veneti restaurant near Cavendish Square; and Stefano Bergamin, from Castelfranco Veneto, who owns Bacco in Richmond.

Two clothes shops with owners from the Veneto recorded even higher levels of consumption than restaurants: Suomi

La Valle served it in his wife's dress shop in Knightsbridge, with a slice of the salami he brought in from a friend of his from Asolo called Menegon, who also supplied him with grappa. Suomi, a professional photographer who was associated with an architects' practice, converted everyone to Prosecco. He inspired his friend Lorenzo Berni from the Osteria San Lorenzo with his passion for the wine. The Venetian Leonardo Barolo, an enthusiastic promoter of "Made in Italy" clothing, ordered Prosecco in the restaurants he frequented, in particular Spago restaurant in South Kensington, where he consumed an average of two to three bottles a day. Luckily for him, it was Prosecco, which is a light and diuretic wine.

p. 126, Claudio Pulze was involved with numerous London restaurants, such as Montpeliano, La Spiga, Il Forno, Il Duca, Zafferano, Alloro, Memories of China, Latium and many others. With Franco Zanellato he created Pasta Bar and the A–Z group. Pulze also partnered with Roberto Pisano – a very active Sardinian who later became general manager of the "A to Z" Group. Roberto now successfully runs Edera in Holland Park.

p. 127, Lorenzo Berni arrived in England by chance. He worked on cruise ships, and during one of his trips the ship sank near the English coast because of a fire on board. During his stay in London, while waiting to return to Italy, he found a job at the Cumberland Hotel near Marble Arch, and settled in London. In 2013 Lorenzo and his daughter Marina franchised a new San Lorenzo in the Taj Lands End hotel in Mumbai, India.

p. 129, Mara died in April 2012. Her sons Ghigo and Paolo manage San Lorenzo Fuoriporta in Wimbledon, while her daughter Marina works with her father.

NOTES

p. 130, La Taverna was sold in April 2014, after fifty-two years. Today it is a Greek restaurant called The Real Greek.

p. 133, Gianni Bucci junior runs his own restaurant, Il Frantoio, on the King's Road.

p. 135, Gino Taddei, following the concept which lay behind Cibo and L'Altro, was later involved with Il Posto, La Collina, Trenta and Il Giardino, all in London. Prosecco was offered as an aperitif in all these restaurants.

p. 137, Rose Gray died in 2010. Ossie Gray left the River Café the same year to run his own restaurant, The Brackenbury, in Hammersmith.

p. 138, Florians was sold in 2007. Arnie Onisto is now a gardener, while Franco Papa, together with his friend and fellow Sicilian Salvatore Di Bartolo, works in the distribution of Italian wines. In 2018 Franco Papa, in partnership with Simon Piovesan, reopened Florians.

p. 140, Prosecco was introduced to The Walnut Tree by Bill Baker in 1990. Franco Taruschio was Bill's partner in the distribution company Reid Wines.

p. 141, Franco and Ann Taruschio are busy raising funds to support the hospice in Abergavenny.

p. 147, One day Domenico Taravella was arrested in his restaurant and spent a night in jail. In fact it was a stunt, organized to raise funds for charity. His friends were invited to "ransom" him and get him released. This hoax enabled Domenico to raise £6,000 to support a local hospital.

p. 147, Cipriani, Arrigo, *Prigioniero di una stanza a Venezia*, p. 24.

p. 148, To make a Bellini: 1/3 fresh peach juice; 2/3 sparkling wine, Prosecco or champagne. This cocktail has become enormously popular over the years. It was first

233

made by Giuseppe Cipriani in 1948, and called Bellini because at that time an important exhibition of the painter Giovanni Bellini, was just opening at the Doge's Palace in Venice. This drink is one of the classics of Harry's Bar; its pleasant taste has led to its success with a sophisticated public all over the world. It can be drunk at almost any hour of the day, and is especially good in summer. See Marino Marini, *Bar Story. Destinazione shaker* (Bologna: Videodidattica, 1993).

The winemaker Canella di San Donà di Piave (Venice) has acquired the rights to the name for producing bottled Bellinis.

p. 148, Carpaccio is a slice of raw meat. Today "carpaccio" has acquired a wider meaning internationally, and covers any product cut into thin slices.

p. 148, Federico Bonetti, from Bergamo, tells the story of how, as soon as he arrived in London, he went to the Osteria San Lorenzo to ask for work. The manager Lucio Altana quickly sent him away, because he didn't need new staff, but said he could try again in the future. After a fortnight Federico turned up again at San Lorenzo. Lucio said, "Haven't I seen you before?" Federico replied: "I was here two weeks ago. I'd like to work for the best restaurants." So Lucio said, "All right, I'll take you on, because you've got the right attitude."

p. 152, Franco Merloni died in 2003.

p. 154, In July 2014 Roberto Gardetto, Lorenzo Castiglioni and the chef Silvano Mazzoli took over the management of The Hurtwood Inn, a pub and restaurant in Peaslake, among the wooded hills of Surrey.

p. 156, The new Casa Carlo closed in 2013.

p. 160, Paolo Mancassola introduced the *pearà* sauce. *Pearà* means "peppery" in the dialect of the Veneto. It is the local Veronese sauce which accompanies boiled meats. Possible ingredients for the recipe include beef marrow, butter or olive oil, stale breadcrumbs, beef stock, black pepper, salt and grated cheese. Today Paolo runs Di Paolo in Gerrards Cross, a wealthy area of Buckinghamshire.

Regular customers at Valentino included Remo Nardone of Enotria; Lee Hoo Fook, owner of the restaurant named after him in Soho, the first Chinese restaurateur to include Prosecco on his wine list; Booth, who runs the Thai restaurant Bangkok in South Kensington; and Enzo Diacono, an architect from the Veneto.

p. 160, Doriano Castellani has close ties to the Veneto, and loves Prosecco in all its forms – *frizzante*, spumante, Cartizze. He has promoted it outside London, in Kent, where clients tend to be less up to date with the latest products, but are happy to follow the suggestions of the waiters. Doriano has been involved with Amalfi in Soho, Il Falconiere in Chelsea, and Roberto's, Don Giovanni, Zi' Teresa and Lugana in Kent.

p. 161, Geoff Hayward owns and manages Virginia Hayward, a company which specializes in gift hampers and includes Italian wines in its catalogue.

p. 161, Gino Ruocco was survived by his wife Daniela, who taught Italian at a school in Kent, and his daughter Cristiana. Among his clients were La Bicicletta, owned by the Sardinian Alberto Piras; Giuseppe Marmo's restaurant Peppe; the distributor Guido Taliana; and Rinaldo Pierini's La Genova.

p. 162, In the past, the terms *vite* ("vine") and *vita* ("life") were thought to be specially connected. The old people in a village near Treviso remember the parish priest Don Pietro Battocchio, who knew Latin, often saying to his congregation in the sermons he preached: "I am the vine and you are the *pampani*." In the dialect of the Veneto, *pampano* has two meanings: it can refer to a stupid or naive person and also to vine stems which have to be cut away because they produce no fruit.

PART IV

p. 168, Vinitaly is the annual wine fair held in Verona, usually at the beginning of spring. It is an opportunity for more than 4,000 producers to introduce themselves to dealers, journalists and importers from all over the world. The 2014 fair was attended by more than 150,000 visitors. Over four days the producers convey the enormous excitement in the world of wine. Long-term attendees at the fair recall how the event has grown, with a steady increase in the number of exhibitors and visitors, and greater coverage in the press and on television. In the past, Prosecco had a display in the Veneto stand, among the exhibitors representing the wines of Valdobbiadene and Conegliano. In more recent years, Prosecco has become the lead wine for winemakers and bottlers in regions such as Trentino, Piedmont, Emilia-Romagna, Tuscany and others.

The fair reflects the remarkable growth of the wine sector in Italy. The number of producers has grown, and the quality of the wines has improved, as has the presentation of the stands and the attractiveness of the bottles on display. What is unchanged is the organization of the fair, which remains poor, and inconvenient for foreign visitors, to the extent that one has to wonder whether the lovely city of Verona is really the best place to host an exhibition of this size. An Italian distributor who works in Glasgow, and who has been visiting Vinitaly for over twenty years, in 2015 said that "The fair in Verona is a perfect picture of what Italy is like. You start by having to book a hotel fifty kilometres away. The transport system is inadequate, and you have to get to the fair by car. There are lots of car parks, but after queuing for ages we end up paying to use the car park for the fruit-and-veg market. It's like a quarry full of cement mixers, and there's an old disused factory as well. To get to the exit on foot you have to walk along a stony dirt road. If it's a sunny day your shoes get covered in dust. If it's wet you get splashed with mud from all the puddles. Once you're out of the car park, you cross the road by climbing a noisy temporary bridge built out of scaffolding. Finally, after a couple of glasses of wine, the fair begins and you forget the unpleasantness, until it's time to join the long queue to get out of the car park."

p. 169, Val D'Oca is part of Cantina Produttori di Valdobbiadene. It was founded in 1952 and today includes over six hundred members, including farmers, viticulturists and producers. They've supplied Prosecco to many major wineries. Franco Varaschin, the current chairman, says: "Directly or indirectly, we have been in the British market from the very beginning."

p. 169, Production and sales data at the end of 2017 (total production in 75cl bottles): Prosecco DOC: 439,700,895. UK market consumption: 129,590,930, i.e. over 29% of the total. Prosecco DOCG Valdobbiadene Conegliano: 94,413,385. UK market: 5,504,127 (5.8%). Prosecco

DOCG Asolo e Montello: 10,674,393. The author hazards that, in addition to the estimated 135,000,000 bottles of Prosecco imported into the UK in 2017, at least an additional 10% of illegally imported bottles should be added. This "illegal" Prosecco can be found especially in cash-and-carry shops, off-licences and restaurants.

p. 169, The data consultant Paolo Nolasco said, in 2015: "In its large-scale distribution in the UK, Prosecco underwent an important growth until 2008–09, achieving a high level of visibility (about 5% of all Italian products). After 3–4 years of consolidation, in 2013–14 there was a new surge, which doubled its previous level and brought it into line with markets traditionally more favourable to Prosecco, such as Austria and Germany.

"The major difference with these markets is in the preferred version of the product: in the UK 95% of sales are of the spumante, while in Austria and Germany there's a predominance of *frizzante*, with a market share of about 60% (a third with the string, the rest of the bottles having the embedded cork or the mushroom-shaped one).

"Allowing for import duty, there's a saving of 60p a bottle on *frizzanti*, which could be reinvested in marketing the product, especially if the string design – which offers many publicity opportunities – is chosen. The buyers probably think this saving is too low to choose *frizzanti* over the higher-profile spumanti."

In general, *frizzante* sales have plummeted. All the efforts and the publicity activities of the three consortia, as well as those of individual companies, are focused on the image of spumante, for the simple reason that *frizzante* is regarded as a lower-quality version of Prosecco, and there is no demand for it.

p. 170, Master of Wine is a prestigious qualification. It is obtained after three years of studying all aspects of wine. In 2014 there were over 300 Masters of Wine.

p. 170, It is not only wine that receives personal endorsements on the label, but products such as pasta and oil.

p. 173, There are more economical, suitable and widespread methods of winemaking. In the European community, the word "wine" is associated with the pressing of grapes and the fermentation of fresh juice. In Great Britain there is confusion about the use of the terminology. "English wine" refers to wine produced from grapes grown on English and Welsh soil in accordance with European rules. However, "British wines" can be produced with juice concentrate from other countries. Producing these requires only the addition of sugar and water. The British Government shows little interest in regulating or clarifying this practice, as long as the producers pay the duty on alcohol. Once these concentrates came from Italy. Now it is more economical to acquire them from other countries. One of the leading producers of "British-made wine" is Continental Quattro Stagioni, a long-established distributor of Italian food products, whose owners are Marino Bevilacqua and his son Sandro, from Le Marche.

According to the Wine Standard Board, there are over 350 vineyards producing wine on English soil, chiefly in the counties of Sussex, Kent, Surrey and Hampshire. Seventeen vineyards are spread across Wales. The total cultivated area is around 1,500 hectares. The amount of white wine produced is 20,184 hectolitres, while the figure for red wine stands at 5,083 hectolitres (2006). Among the varieties cultivated are Pinot Noir and Chardonnay, used principally for sparkling wines. English and British wines represent less than 1% of consumption in the domestic market.

p. 178, Gilles de la Bassetière, *président-directeur général* of the firm Champagne de Venoge, points out that it was during the recent meeting of the CIVC (2014) that Prosecco was mentioned for the first time. CIVC is the Comité Interprofessionnel du vin de Champagne, an organization which controls the production, distribution and promotion of wines from the Champagne region and includes producers, cooperatives and dealers under the direction of the French Government.

p. 178, As a salesman, Roberto Simeone was one of the first to see the importance of consumers of wine outside restaurants. Among his best clients, he numbers Oxford University and Guy's and St Thomas's Hospitals.

p. 180, Cipriani, Arrigo, *Harry's Bar, a Venetian Legend*, p. 14.

p. 182, The first restaurant owned by Rinaldo Mollura was La Cage Imaginaire. Rinaldo had included Prosecco on the wine list at La Cage Imaginaire, even though it was a French concern. When asked, "Why a French restaurant?" Rinaldo answered that back then the image of French cuisine was more serious. He has recently acquired his fifth Italian restaurant and devotes at least two hours a day to boxing and tennis. He has discovered that in a business as demanding as the restaurant trade, his leisure time helps him to come up with new ideas: "Otherwise I'd go mad."

p. 183, Fratelli La Bufala is a chain of Italian pizzerias which has opened branches in England and aims to expand further. Enzo Oliveri is a partner and manages operations in Great Britain.

p. 183, Andrea Riva has always run Riva along similar lines, but its success is attributable to Andrea's powerful personality rather than to a particular operating model.

p. 186, *Londra Sera* is a London-based weekly newspaper which reports events and stories from the Italian community in Britain. Its founder and editor is Tommaso Bruccoleri. In 2012, Salvatore Mancuso, a former colleague on *Londra Sera*, started *La Notizia*, a twice-yearly magazine dealing with Italian matters.

p. 187, A joke overheard in 2009 in a bar in Treviso.

p. 191, Roberto Scalzo and his siblings bought Patisserie Valerie in 1987.

p. 194, The three consortia are Consorzio del Prosecco DOCG di Conegliano e Valdobbiadene, Consorzio del Prosecco DOCG Asolo e Montello and Consorzio del Prosecco DOC.

p. 196, Virgilio Gennaro claimed that it is the simplicity of Prosecco that has introduced many consumers to sparkling wines.

p. 196, Alessio Fuso is a dealer with international experience working for the San Margherita Group.

p. 199, Prosecco's popularity has favoured a market run by large-scale buyers who set the prices. Satisfying them means damaging the prospects of Prosecco.

p. 199, Maria Luisa Dalla Costa entered the world of Prosecco at a very early age. She grew up in Paolo Bisol's Ruggeri Spa, which produces one of Valdobbiadene's historic labels, and worked there for twenty-four years, mostly in sales. She later became sales manager for Col Vetoraz, where she worked for eight years, before joining the commercial management team at Merotto in 2006. Having thus spent about forty years working in the field of high-quality Prosecco, she is jokingly called Lady Prosecco by friends and colleagues.

p. 199, In Veneto dialect "*riva*" (plural "*rive*") indicates a plot of land with a vineyard on a hillside.

p. 200, In July 2009, under the new regulations, the historic area of Conegliano-Valdobbiadene was given distinctive terminology to make this difference clear: first DOCG, then the word "Superiore" and lastly the term "Rive". On the scale of quality, the topmost rung is occupied by Cartizze, with its extremely limited production. However, when one speaks of Prosecco Superiore, the appellation *Rive*, synonymous with the French *cru*, refers to vineyards cultivated on the particularly steep and precipitous slopes of a high hill.

p. 200, Anyone who wishes to learn more about the soil composition in the areas producing Prosecco is recommended to read Diego Tomasi, Federica Gaiotti and Gregory V. Jones's *The Power of the Terroir: The Case Study of Prosecco Wine* (Basel: Springer, 2013).

p. 202, It is easy to understand the lack of sympathy towards Italian governments and politicians, who offer no response to the needs of the population.

p. 202, The case of the banker Amedeo Giannini in California is well known. In San Francisco, in 1908, after the hardships of the earthquake which had shocked the economy, Giannini financed the Italian community's recovery by offering loans based on no more security than a handshake. In due course the loans were repaid and Giannini's Italian Bank achieved such importance that it later merged with the Bank of America. One can learn from this example: solidarity brings advantages to all, while exploitation and criminality foster incomprehension, hatred and suffering.

p. 202, This happened in the USA during the Second World War. In that situation of crisis, Italian immigrants were given an ultimatum and told to choose whose side they were on. Many declared themselves to be American, ready to fight against Italy.

The author regrets that he was not able to explore and report the experience of many other Italians who exerted a great influence in promoting Prosecco in the United Kingdom. He invites those who have a story to tell to send it to the following email address: alfieridelprosecco@gmail.com. It will be considered for future editions of the book.